# NEW YORK NEON

# NEW YORK NEON

THOMAS E. RINALDI

W. W. Norton & Company
New York • London

For information about permission to reproduce
selections from this book, write to
Permissions, W. W. Norton & Company, Inc.,
500 Fifth Avenue, New York, NY 10110

For information about special discounts for bulk
purchases, please contact W. W. Norton
Special Sales at specialsales@wwnorton.com or
800-233-4830

Manufacturing through Asia Pacific
Book design by Modern Good
Digital production: Joe Lops
Production manager: Leeann Graham

Library of Congress Cataloging-in-Publication Data

Rinaldi, Thomas E.
New York neon / Thomas E. Rinaldi. — 1st ed.
    p. cm.
Includes bibliographical references and index.
ISBN 978-0-393-73341-9 (pbk.)
1. Neon signs—New York (State)—New York—
History. I. Title.
GT3911.N72N475 2013
302.23—dc23
                                        2012011406


ISBN: 978-0-393-73341-9 (pbk.)

W. W. Norton & Company, Inc., 500 Fifth Avenue,
New York, N.Y. 10110
www.wwnorton.com

W. W. Norton & Company Ltd., Castle House, 75/76
Wells Street, London W1T 3QT

FOR MY PARENTS,
JOSEPH AND MARY RINALDI,
WHO SHOWED ME THE CITY

# CONTENTS

WAVERLY

D'AIUTO

KATZ'S DELICATESSEN

TOM'S RESTAURANT

Cheyenne

DINER

CLOVER

DELICATESSEN

PARK

# PREFACE

More than anything, the signs drew me because they seemed poised to disappear. Photographers are often transfixed by the ephemeral. I have always found myself especially susceptible to a documentary instinct. Before undertaking this project, I co-authored *Hudson Valley Ruins*, a book that sought to document threatened historic sites in the Hudson River Valley. As with *New York Neon*, a key motivation was to record something being lost without due recognition of its significance.

Once an ordinary feature of the city streets, by the 1980s these old neon signs stood out in New York as antiques. When as a child I visited the city in those years, the signs caught my eye as curiosities. Moving to New York in 2004, I noted with regret that many had vanished. Those that survived fascinated me as objects that gave great character to the streetscape. Moreover, they almost invariably marked the spot of venerable old neighborhood haunts—bars, restaurants, drugstores—that had been around for generations. I made a habit of visiting these places as often as I could.

I set about photographing New York's dwindling number of old neon signs in September 2006 and spent the next five years seeking out signs and taking the photographs in this book. I limited my scope to exposed-tube neon signs in the five boroughs of the City of New York. With very few exceptions, the signs included here date to before 1970, when the character of typical storefront signs in New York changed with the ascendance of new materials and techniques in the sign industry.

Taking my inspiration from popular nocturnal photomontages created in the 1920s and '30s, I began by photographing the signs illuminated at night, with my camera's aperture set about two f-stops below what my light meter told me it should be, so that the photograph captured only the neon tubes against a black background. I soon began trying to include more of the context around the signs, which allowed me to expand my scope to relic signs that no longer light and the sheet metal details behind the neon tubes that are key to the appeal of these old signs.

Most of the photographs were made at dusk, around 8 p.m. in the summer, 4 p.m. in the winter, just before the streetlights come on, when there is sufficient ambient light to capture the signs in context without overexposing the glow. This gave me a narrow window of about twenty-five minutes each evening in which to shoot, making it nearly impossible to photograph more than one sign a night. I made a handful of the earlier photographs with slide film, but the demanding nature of the project soon forced me to move to digital equipment.

Picture books of old neon signs are not a new idea. To go beyond simple photographic documentation, I sought to trace the provenance of the signs by identifying a maker and installation date for as many as possible. This proved extraordinarily difficult. In theory, the information should be on record at the city's Department of Buildings. But in most cases the records were missing or incomplete. So I telephoned the business owners whose services the signs advertise. A daunting task at first, this proved to be perhaps the most interesting and rewarding phase of the project, even if the shopkeepers themselves rarely could tell me what I wanted to know.

Ultimately this undertaking has been a race against time. The struggle to keep up with the alarming rate at which the signs continue to disappear has been as much frustration as motivation. Time and again I trekked halfway across the city only to find a sign vanished, even if it still existed in the virtual reality of Google Street View. The disappearance of the signs is one of many indicators of the pace of change in contemporary New York. This theme has been the genesis of many recent projects, of which this is but one. I have endeavored to minimize overlap with these other works, and I hope that my modest book will contribute something original and meaningful to the vast library of books dedicated to this great city.

# ACKNOWLEDGMENTS

This work reflects the great measure of assistance, counsel, and support I received from dozens of people who helped me along the way. First and foremost, I am grateful to Andrew Scott Dolkart of the Graduate School of Architecture, Planning, and Historic Preservation at Columbia University, and to Nancy Green at W. W. Norton for seeing potential in this project at an early stage. I am indebted to Corinne Meli, Amy Sonricker, and Rob Yasinsac for proofreading the proposal; to Paul Shaw for his advice on type designs; to Ross Savedge and Allen Shifrin for helping to edit the manuscript; and especially to my parents for support both emotional and material, without which this project could not have come to pass.

I thank my friends, mentors, and new acquaintances who contributed advice, moral support, or otherwise humored me in this off-beat hobby: Yiannis Arramides, Marcos Bayas, Steven Chin, Eric Corwin, Charles and Marilyn Dorato, David Freeland, Christopher Gray, Justin Greenawalt, Bob Kornfeld, Mary McLeod, Jeremiah Moss, Kett Murphy, Tara Rasheed, John Reddick, Ross Savedge, Myrna Suárez, and Kerensa Wood, among others. I owe a special debt of thanks to Anthony Clark, Jill Perrius, and Allen Shifrin, who spent long nights traversing Brooklyn, Queens, and the Bronx with me on a seemingly interminable scavenger hunt for odd bits of New York's commercial archaeology.

This project benefited tremendously from archival resources whose pleasant guardians made my research significantly less painful than it might have been without their patience and help. For their assistance navigating and providing access to these materials, I thank Ken Cobb at the Municipal Archives of the City of New York; Susan Crete at the New-York Historical Society; Diane Fuller at Consolidated Edison; Erin Schreiner at the Avery Architectural and Fine Arts Library at Columbia University; Tod Swormstedt at the American Sign Museum; Wade Swormstedt at *Signs of the Times* magazine; Harold Wallace at the National Museum of American History at the Smithsonian Institution; and, most of all, Will Britten and the staff of the Science, Industry, and Business Library of the New York Public Library, which at times felt like a second home.

Seeking out and photographing the signs featured in this book brought me into contact with the men and women who pay the bills to keep them lit. New York's small business owners are a tough lot, and they don't always take kindly to camera-wielding strangers; one or two of them more or less told me to get the hell off their property. Luckily, most shopkeepers I spoke with expressed surprising enthusiasm for this book once they learned what I was up to, and meeting the faces behind some of New York's most venerable businesses was one of the real pleasures of this undertaking. To Stanley Bard of the Chelsea Hotel, Richie Collins of Capitol Fishing Tackle Co., Frank Cuttita Jr. of the Clover Delicatessen, Antonio DeSilva of Restaurant Rocco, Frank DeVito of DeVito Paint and Wallpaper, Fedora Dorato of Fedora Restaurant, Herman Hochberg of Queens Liquor and Wine Store, John Logue Jr. of Hinsch's Confectionary, Rita Miller of Miller's Prescriptions, Miriam Moccia of McKey's Liquors, Pietro Mosconi of Monte's Trattoria, Sal and Joe Scognamillo of Patsy's Italian Restaurant, Moe Stein of Frank's Sports Shop, Stuart Tarabour of Forager's Market in Brooklyn, Pat Vitiello of the Queen Marie Italian Restaurant, Buddy Zeccardi of Caffé Roma, Robert Zerilli of Veniero's Pasticceria, and everyone else who turned the lights on for me, I offer my sincere thanks.

I am indebted to the numerous veterans of New York's neon sign business who gave generously of their time to educate me on a subject about which I knew little at the outset. Steven Higger (United Sign Systems), Al Higger (Silverescent Neon Sign Co.), and Justin Langsner (La Salle Sign Corp.) spent hours on the phone sharing old stories and putting faces to names. Robbie Ingui, a second-generation neon sign maker from Artistic Neon Inc., and Max Langhurst, a neon artist, invited me to spend an evening in Ridgewood, Queens, to gain a firsthand understanding of the fine craft of neon glass bending. Later, it was a true pleasure to spend a day with Robbie's parents, Gasper and Carmela Ingui, at their home in upstate New York, learning the ins and outs of a difficult trade in which there is never a dull moment, over heaping portions of home-made lasagna and braciole that alone would have been worth the trip (Mrs. Ingui sent me home with enough leftovers to live on for a week). My thanks also to Paul Boegemann of Paul Signs, Harvey Brooks and Ralph Garcia at Spectrum Signs, Jimmy Coccaro of Super Neon Lights in Bensonhurst, Jeff Friedman of Let There Be Neon in Tribeca, Meryl Gaitan of Midtown Sign Services, Tama Starr of Artkraft Strauss, Pat Tommaso of Manhattan Neon, Mike Lettera and Jack Saraceno at the Lettera Sign and Electric Co., and Lenny and Rose Weisenthal of Louis Striar Inc., for helping me get up to speed.

Without question, the high points for me were those days when I had the pleasure of meeting the people who made the signs pictured in this book and hearing their remarkable stories. Not only was this experience essential to what I had hoped to accomplish in this undertaking—recording the largely undocumented and generally misunderstood provenance of these signs—but I got to meet some remarkable New Yorkers. I hope I have done justice to the important role they have played in making New York the city we know and love.

ABOVE Some businesses go to great lengths to keep their old signs on the premises. Originally opened in the former Holland Hotel on West 42nd Street, the Holland Bar and Coffee Shop installed this sign over its door in 1949. When circumstances forced the bar to find a new home some forty years later, its owners took the sign with them. Too large to hang over the bar's new storefront, they found room for it inside, over the bar. An urn nested between the letters O and L holds the ashes of longtime regular Charlie O'Connor.

# INTRODUCTION

⇨ Few elements of the built environment elicit such strong feelings as neon signs do. In New York, old neon signs symbolize an era whose remnants are disappearing rapidly. The quickening pace of physical change in the city has stirred controversy and consternation manifested in books, blogs, documentary films, and discussion groups with names such as "The Suburbanization of New York" and "The Vanishing City." All pose essentially the same question: has New York gone too far in cleaning up?

The dwindling number of old neon signs—and the venerable businesses they advertise—is an indicator of the city's changing character. These signs often announced some of New York's most stalwart commercial institutions: Ratner's, the Second Avenue Deli, the Times Square Howard Johnson's, McHale's, the P&G Bar: when these places pack it in, their signs disappear with them.

Ironically, the impetus to preserve old neon signs has come in part from the same kinds of civic groups that once called for their prohibition: some signs now protected by New York's Landmarks Commission could not be installed under current zoning ordinances. Yet when neon first appeared, it was as much identified with the onslaught of new upon old as it is now of old yielding to new. In the early part of the twentieth century, neon signs (and their incandescent predecessors) posed an affront to the traditional character of the streetscapes they transformed. For the half-century that they dominated the urban landscape, neon signs were both loved and hated like perhaps no other elements of the built environment. The historical inconsistencies of popular attitudes toward neon reveal much about how humans relate to their built surroundings.

My mission in this book is two-fold. First, by focusing on signs made before new materials and design ideas fundamentally changed the character of typical outdoor advertising displays by the late 1960s, I assess the significance of New York's historic

All in the family: in changing times, old neon signs have come to symbolize the "soul" of the city in the twenty first century. ABOVE Justin Langsner worked with his father in making the Papaya King signs in 1964;

CENTER Fedora Dorato, here photographed by Myrna Suárez, ran the restaurant that bore her name for more than 60 years; ABOVE RIGHT Robbie Ingui learned the art of neon tube bending from his father, Gasper.

neon signs and create a record of their design. I concentrate not on the enormous "spectaculars" of Times Square, which have already been well documented, but on the smaller, far more prevalent "on-premise" storefront signs that have survived much longer. I treat the city as an open-air museum of signs by curating and documenting these objects as museum pieces. Second, in exploring the conflicted sentiment toward the signs, I point to intangible qualities whose presence, though seldom acknowledged, is crucial to the livability of our built environment. A note: throughout the text, I use the term "neon sign" generically to describe luminous tube commercial signs that use noble gases such as argon, helium, and xenon in addition to neon.

# EVOLUTION

⇨ Neon signs are not unique to New York. They came to America by way of Europe and went on to proliferate along small-town Main Streets and the Las Vegas Strip, Route 66, and the highway interchange. Yet having come of age on Broadway and multiplied by the tens of thousands throughout the five boroughs, neon became a signature part of the New York streetscape by the middle

years of the twentieth century. The signs are there in the New York of Berenice Abbott, Walker Evans, Andreas Feininger, Frank O'Hara, and Langston Hughes, and almost any given film noir of the same period. They were touchstones of the city's twentieth-century identity.

Illuminated signs of various forms preceded the advent of neon by centuries. Clever business owners devised primitive modes of illuminated advertising long before the commercial availability of electricity. In his 1850 travelogue of New York nightlife, *New York by Gas-Light*, George Foster wrote of "painted lanterns" hung by the doors of oyster bars, and of "Drummond Lights" (or lime lights) that drew customers to establishments ranging from P. T. Barnum's American Museum on Broadway to Butter-cake Dick's, an all-night "underground newsboy's eating-house" off Park Row.

Internally lit "shadow-box" or "silhouette" signs proliferated with the introduction of gas illumination in the first decades of the nineteenth century (first in London in 1807, and later in New York by 1824). Such signs could be fashioned from a simple oblong wooden box, its prominent faces perforated with letters or shapes that could be made to glow at night, jack-o'-lantern-style, when lit from within. The advent of gaslight facilitated the development of

ABOVE A typical gaslit sign, as illustrated in an 1870s catalog of gaslight fixtures by Mitchell, Vance & Co. Illuminated signs became increasingly common during the gaslight era.

ABOVE 1930s photographs showing (clockwise from top left) Eighth Avenue, Delancey Street and 125th Street in Manhattan, and Main Street in Flushing, Queens. Neon Signs were a signature part of the New York streetscape by World War II. Photographs by P.L. Sperr.

a small industry specializing in the production of illuminated signs by the last quarter of the century. Gaslit signs advertised hotels, restaurants, and especially theaters, such as Tony Pastor's New York music halls. To prevent accidental fires, metal replaced wood as the sign maker's preferred material. Special mechanisms called "gaswinkers" allowed signs to flash on and off automatically. Sign panels could be fitted with "jeweled" or opalescent glass lenses. Production of gaslit signs continued into the first years of the twentieth century.

The introduction of Edison's incandescent lamp in 1879 spelled the end for gaslight, which many regarded as dirty, hot, and dangerous. Signs using incandescent bulbs appeared even before Edison established the world's first commercial system of electrical distribution in New York in September 1882. William J. Hammer, an Edison associate, devised what is considered the first electric sign for the International Electrical Exhibition of 1882, held at London's Crystal Palace. Its bulbs (with filaments of bamboo) formed the name EDISON.

The world's first large electrified commercial billboard appeared in July 1892. Facing out over Madison Square in New York from the rear wall of the Cumberland Hotel, it advertised the pleasures of places reachable by the Long Island Rail Road:

BUY HOMES ON LONG ISLAND / SWEPT BY OCEAN BREEZES. The "Ocean Breezes" sign disappeared by 1895, replaced by a display advertising the New York Times, and later by one promoting Heinz pickles. The "pickle sign," as it was called, vanished when the site was cleared to make way for the Flatiron Building, completed in 1903. By then, though, electric signs had become a familiar part of the New York landscape: references to Broadway as the "Great White Way" appeared as early as 1902.

Electrified off-premise advertising billboards (signs advertising goods and services not necessarily available in the immediate vicinity of the sign itself) appeared with ever-greater sophistication. These sprang up especially at the "squares" formed where Broadway's diagonal crossed the streets and avenues of the Manhattan grid. By the early 1900s, one New York firm—the O. J. Gude Company—took the lead in the production of increasingly complex illuminated "spectaculars" (the term "spectacular," shorthand for "spectacular display," quickly became standard industry parlance for the largest electric signs). From their birthplace at Madison Square, where Broadway crosses 23rd Street, the spectaculars made their way uptown to Herald Square (at 34th Street), eventually reaching Columbus Circle (at 59th Street) and beyond. The global electric billboard phenomenon

ABOVE A 1948 photograph showing nightclubs on West 52nd Street in Manhattan. "On premise" signs for restaurants and other businesses made an impact on streets throughout the city. Photograph by William Gottlieb.

soon centered on Longacre Square, the intersection of Broadway, Seventh Avenue, and West 42nd Street, renamed Times Square when the New York Times opened its new headquarters building there in 1904.

Though "spectacular," most off-premise signs (electrified or not) typically survived no more than a few years. (Two Times Square spectaculars—the famous smoking Camel cigarettes sign of 1942 and the Canadian Club whiskey spectacular of 1952—each survived in essentially the same form for twenty-three years, setting what is probably the endurance record for off-premise electric spectaculars on Broadway.) On-premise electric signs, those situated on or immediately adjacent to the premises of what they advertised, proved longer-lived and far more numerous. While the great electric billboards of Times Square and elsewhere have attracted more attention in both contemporary and historical studies, the smaller, more common on-premise signs advertising storefronts, restaurants, and theaters made a greater impact on the character of the urban landscape in New York and in cities and towns around the globe.

Miner's Fifth Avenue Theatre in New York installed one of the world's first recorded on-premise outdoor electric signs in 1894. By 1917, Arthur Williams of the New York Edison Company noted that the number of electric signs in New York had reached "many thousands" and that permit applications for new electric signs were being filed at a rate of about two hundred every month. Williams found electric signs advertising playhouses and moving picture houses, candy stores and pharmacists, delicatessens, restaurants and lunchrooms, shoe stores, tailors and pawnshops, banks, insurance companies and department stores, and large hotels—all kinds of businesses, throughout the city.

The most basic electric signs, sometimes called "panel signs" or "panel reflector signs," were simple signboards lit with incandescent bulbs housed in hooded fixtures. Shadow-box signs, meanwhile, proved readily adaptable to electric light and grew increasingly common. Finally, many sign makers used incandescent lamps to great effect by leaving the bulbs themselves exposed. To reduce glare and improve legibility, makers of these exposed lamp signs soon adopted the practice of fitting metal flanges to the edges of letters or shapes, thus creating what became known as the "trough" or "channel letter."

Electric power utilities played an important role in the proliferation of illuminated signs through the first decades of the twentieth century. The New York Edison Company established an Electric Sign Bureau for this purpose before World War I. America's

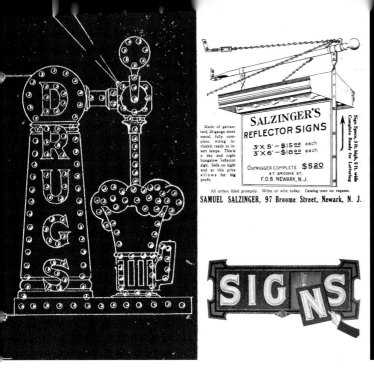

ABOVE Early 1920s advertisements from *Signs of the Times* showing panel reflector (above right), opalescent glass (bottom right), and exposed bulb signs (above left).

ABOVE, OPPOSITE New York Edison helped stimulate demand for electric signs by holding annual "Electric Sign Shows" beginning in 1921.

entry into the war brought energy conservation measures that forced businesses to dim their signs for the duration of hostilities. After 1918, New York Edison went into high gear, holding annual "electric sign shows," beginning in 1921. In 1923 it undertook the first of several annual "electric sign surveys," for which it canvassed all of Manhattan below 135th Street, inventorying every electric sign within the boundaries of its distribution network.

"What makes New York's Great White Way light as day at midnight?" asked a reporter covering Edison's first sign survey: "It is the restaurateurs and the tobacco merchants who are responsible for Manhattan's bright lights." The survey counted 1,360 electric signs on Broadway alone (Eighth Avenue came in at a distant second, with 454). Signs for restaurants were the most numerous; movie theaters ranked ninth, after dentists and doctors, shoe stores, drugstores, and confectionaries. Bars and liquor stores, having been forced underground with the enactment of Prohibition, were out of the running. In their stead, undertakers and churches had also turned to electric signs to drum up business. The 1923 survey tallied 9,577 electric signs that used upward of one million incandescent bulbs. The total rose to 18,958 by 1927. Another survey found 750 neon signs in New York in the same year.

## ENTER NEON

⇨ Unlike incandescent lamps, which produce light by passing an electric current through a filament until it heats to the point of glowing, neon lamps work by providing a sealed environment through which an electrical current can "arc" (or jump) across a gap between electrodes to complete a circuit. Light is produced by the excitement of electrons as the gas within the tube conducts the electrical charge across the gap. Neon was neither the first nor the last gas employed in "gas discharge lamps," as this mode of illumination is known.

Experiments based on this technology date at least as far back as the seventeenth century but reached a milestone in 1857 with the "Geissler tube," a device developed by the German physicist Heinrich Geissler (1814–1879), in which a constant but faint luminous glow was produced in a glass tube filled with a rarefied gas and charged with electricity. The Geissler tube became a popular novelty item in Europe and the United States during the last quarter of the nineteenth century: its glass tubes were typically formed into delicate spirals and other elaborate shapes. But the short life of the tube and the dimness of the light that was

produced effectively limited the Geissler tube's potential for signs or other commercial applications.

In the early 1890s, gas discharge lamps became the subject of experiments by prominent inventors, including Edison, Nikola Tesla, and others. The most significant progress came at the hands of an Edison associate, D. McFarlan Moore (1869–1936), who started his own company to develop an improved luminous gas discharge lamp that he hoped would succeed the incandescent light bulb for conventional applications. "The incandescent electric lamp of to-day hardly satisfies the demand of these progressive times," wrote Moore in 1894: "a new method must succeed it." Neon gas had yet to be discovered, and the "Moore tube light" used common carbon dioxide to produce a pure, white glow. Moore later experimented with other gases such as nitrogen and helium, but for various reasons he did not effectively explore the potential of neon after its discovery in 1898. Nonetheless, his development of practical gas discharge lamps put all the pieces in place for the rise of neon illumination in the years to come.

Moore envisioned the use of his lamps for architectural lighting: "The coming cylinders of light will glow with impunity in the open. . . . In the future, elaborate fixtures will be conspicuously absent." Tesla, who backed Moore, saw the potential of these lamps for exterior applications: "It is hardly too much to say that the beautifying of cities will never be adequately undertaken until the electric light has been improved, or, rather, rendered generally available in its new form."

Moore tubes began to appear in various installations in Newark, New Jersey (where Moore had his laboratory), and in New York City during the 1890s, making their debut in the meeting hall of the American Institute of Electrical Engineers in New York in May 1896. Two years later he mocked up a small, tube-lit chapel inside Stanford White's Madison Square Garden for the Electrical Exhibition of 1898. Permanent Moore tube installations appeared soon afterward in department stores, post offices, and most prominently in the lobby of Madison Square Garden, where they were installed in 1905.

But the Moore tube's most practical commercial application may have been for electrical advertising. Just as Geissler tubes could be bent to form elaborate shapes, Moore shaped his tubes to form letters. In May 1897, he invited the press to his Newark laboratories for the unveiling of recent developments in his system of gas discharge lighting. "The first thing that attracted the

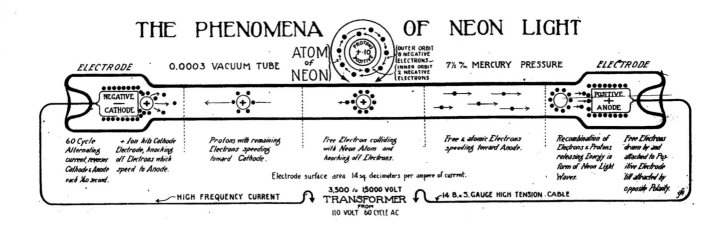

attention was a sign over the door of the hall," noted the *New York Times*:

> It was not like any sign that had ever been put up before in the world's history, either to guide human footsteps, to call attention to the merits of a nostrum, or to herald an epoch-making discovery in science. The word "Welcome" was written above the door in lines of attenuated daylight. It didn't look like gas or calcium light: it didn't resemble electricity. It seemed as if the letters were cut in stencil, and sunlight was streaming through, and silhouetting their outline upon the black night beyond. . . . When one entered the laboratory itself, he observed that one commercial use of the new light was already demonstrated. On one side hung a brilliant sign commending a certain variety of cigarettes, and on the other side was another sign intended to advertise a patent medicine that children were supposed to be continually crying for.

Moore tube signs appeared in growing numbers on the streets of New York over the next few years. "Soon the long-tube installations became commonplace," wrote the neon sign promoter Mel Morris three decades later:

Broadway was soon flanked with a double row of this new type of electrical advertising. One could ride on a Broadway car from Central Park to the Battery in one evening, and have at least one long tube sign in sight all the way. The combined length of these installations would have provided a tube more than four miles in length, giving brilliant white light at a fraction of the cost of unsatisfactory yellow light from [Edison's] old carbon filament lamps.

The trouble with the Moore tube lay in the degradation of the electrodes that delivered current into the tube, as well as the high price of the installations. Moore continued to refine and promote his invention, and he displayed it at the Grand Palais in Paris in 1910. According to one account, Moore's representatives in Paris were approached by Georges Claude (1870–1960), a French scientist then experimenting with industrial applications for gaseous by-products given off by the liquefaction of air, including a newly identified gas called neon. Claude obtained Moore's permission to conduct an experiment, filling a Moore tube with neon gas. The results were encouraging: on November 28, 1910, Claude filed an application for a French patent for "les tubes luminescents au neon," and a year later he submitted an application for a "system of illuminating by

ABOVE A Moore tube sign in New York, c. 1904. The Moore tube lamp paved the way for the ascendance of neon illumination in subsequent decades.

ABOVE Georges Claude's first sale in the United States was to a Packard dealership in California in 1923.

luminescent tubes" at the United States Patent Office. At around the same time, the introduction of tungsten filaments suddenly made incandescent bulbs much more efficient, thus dampening the impetus for Moore's improved electric lamp. Unable to challenge Claude's patents, Moore restored himself to Edison's good graces, sold his own patents to General Electric, and took a position with GE's research laboratories. His tube light was soon relegated to obscure journals of electrical engineering.

The discovery of neon gas had come twelve years before, on June 12, 1898, as a late product of Victorian-era achievement in science and industry, one of several so-called noble (or inert) gases isolated from the air we breathe by the English scientists Sir William Ramsay (1852–1916) and Morris William Travers (1872–1961). In addition to neon, which Ramsay and Travers named for the Greek word for "new," they identified krypton and xenon, which took their names from the Greek words for "hidden" and "stranger," respectively. All were naturally occurring products of experiments in the liquefaction of air.

Upon subjecting each of these gases to spectral analyses in order to make initial assessments of their specific properties, Ramsay and Travers observed that they could be induced to produce a characteristic glow when isolated in a vacuum tube and

then charged with electricity. Neon produced an especially bright glow. "The blaze of crimson light from the tube told its own story, and it was a sight to dwell upon and never to forget," Travers wrote later. "It was worth the struggle of the previous two years . . . for nothing in the world gave a glow such as we had seen." Travers later recalled how he and Ramsay arrived upon the name "neon": "a name for the gas had been suggested by Ramsay's son, Willie, then about thirteen. . . . 'What are you going to call the new gas?' he said, 'I should call it novum.' – 'Neon would sound better,' said his father, and made the entry in his notebook."

The realization of neon's commercial potential came slowly. Ramsay and Travers are said to have employed neon and other gases to create a sign honoring Queen Victoria for the Royal Society of London in June 1898. Moore reportedly had difficulty obtaining enough neon for experiments with his own luminous tubes, and he worked with helium and nitrogen instead. One account credits the first neon advertising sign to two American engineers, John J. Madine and Russell F. Trimble, who fabricated a small neon tube display for the Ingersoll Watch Company of Newark, New Jersey, in 1909.

Of numerous inventors working toward the commercial application of neon tubes in the first decade of the twentieth

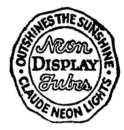

ABOVE Rare view showing one of New York's first Claude Neon signs, which appeared in 1924 to advertise the Loft Candy chain.

ABOVE Georges Claude's patent litigation in the late 1920s did little to dissuade competitors. Other prominent neon sign businesses to appear in New York during this period included Rainbow Light Inc. and American Neon.

century, Georges Claude was triumphant. He owed his success to his ability to resolve persistent impracticalities of the Moore tube by using neon gas and improved electrodes. He envisioned a future for neon light as a competitor to the incandescent bulb for conventional applications. But neon lamps produced a vivid orange-red glow, as Claude acknowledged in his U.S. patent application: "As is known the color of the light emitted by neon when ignited leaves something to be desired owing to its orange tint partaking too much of a red." While Claude pondered a way around this, an assistant, Jacques Fonseque, began marketing neon tubes for electric signs in Paris. Historians provide differing accounts of Claude's first commercial neon sign. In all likelihood it appeared in Paris between 1910 and 1912. Claude came to the United States in 1913, displaying his tubes at the Congress of the Illuminating Society at Pittsburgh, and he tried unsuccessfully to sell his patents (then still pending) to General Electric. The U.S. Patent Office finally issued Claude's neon illumination patents in 1915, but only with significant revisions to his original application.

World War I effectively suspended Claude's progress, but after the war he picked up where he had left off, and neon signs became common in Paris and other European cities. Indicative of the early reception of neon light as an icon of high fashion, Claude's

installations in Paris reportedly included one at Charles Garnier's Opera House in 1919. He made no further significant effort to market neon illumination in the United States until 1924 when, perhaps prompted by his first known American sale—a pair of signs for a Los Angeles Packard dealership in 1923—he organized Claude Neon Lights Inc. in New York City. The company's first neon signs appeared on the streets of the city that year. Early customers included chain stores and large corporations, such as Loft Candies, a soda fountain chain; John Ward, a men's shoe retailer; and Willys-Overland, then one of the largest American automakers.

The growing popularity of neon signs spurred the appearance of competitors in the United States and elsewhere. In a "neon war" that dragged on throughout the 1920s, neon shops continued to appear despite Claude's aggressive legal action against alleged infringement on his patents. One company in particular—Rainbow Lights Inc. of New York—emerged as a formidable opponent. Claude Neon's American profits nonetheless rose to $19 million in 1928, up from $190,000 four years earlier. But with the expiration of his American patents in 1932, the neon business opened to anyone with enough capital to set up shop.

Incandescent bulb signs held on for a few years, but by 1928, neon had swept the country. Apart from their neat and

ABOVE Many New York businesses proudly featured their modern storefronts with neon signs or marquees on advertising postcards during the middle part of the twentieth century.

modern appearance, neon signs reduced the considerable maintenance requirements of incandescent bulb signs. Business owners who had only recently installed incandescent bulb signs now retrofitted them with neon tubes or replaced them outright. Neon consumed much less electricity: the owner of one incandescent bulb sign retrofitted with neon tubes found his sign's energy consumption dropped from 19,350 to 1,400 watt-hours. Within a few years, neon signs grew so numerous in New York and across the American landscape that legions of concerned citizens banded together to protest their installation. As neon's proponents and detractors locked horns over the decades to come, neon signs came to symbolize everything people loved and hated about the modernization of the world around them.

ABOVE The shop of the Higger Sign Co., c. 1950, at 1255 Atlantic Ave. in Bedford-Stuyvesant, Brooklyn.

# ANATOMY OF AN INDUSTRY

⇨ Neon signs were an almost inescapable part of the New York cityscape by the 1930s. Claude's name was synonymous with neon light: some people called the signs "claudeneon," while others mistakenly attributed their invention to someone called "Claude Neon." Claude franchised his patent rights to sign shops around the world, some of which assumed the Claude name themselves: one shop, in Hialeah, Florida, retains the name today. But Claude's predominance in the neon business would not outlive the decade. With the threat of patent litigation no longer looming, small independent sign shops dove into the neon industry faster than Claude could count them.

Prominent Claude-licensed shops in the United States included the Strauss Sign Company of New York, named Artkraft Strauss after a merger in 1936. In its origins, Artkraft Strauss typified the small sign shops that entered the neon business in the 1920s and 1930s, often one-man operations launched by immigrants, especially Italians, Germans, and Eastern European Jews. Some sign makers, like Artkraft Strauss's longtime president Jacob Starr, came to the United States with prior experience in the business. Others came as trained artists who turned to sign painting to put food on the table. The electric sign business likewise offered a good prospect for experienced mechanics, electricians, or otherwise gifted tinkerers. Typically, such a business began small, perhaps making simple paper display cards or gilt wood signboards, and grew into the production of electric signs as the business thrived. Some shops passed to new owners when their founders died, retired, or left the business; others remained in the same families for generations. As businesses of this kind proliferated in the 1930s,

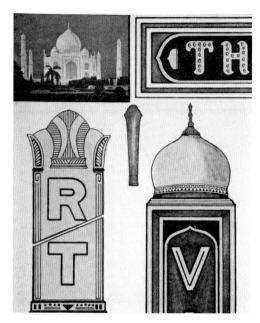

ABOVE An illustration from a 1932 magazine article entitled "Ideas for Electric Display Designs: Where and How to Get Them."

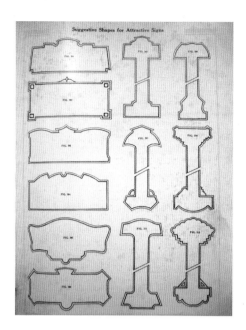

ABOVE A c. 1930 catalog for the Chicago Sign Sales Corp. of Charlotte, North Carolina offered customers this array of "Suggestive Shapes for Attractive Signs."

the Claude name was all but forgotten. Many New York neon shops unionized by the 1930s, and unions exercised almost full control over the industry. After the AFL-CIO merger in 1955, New York neon shops employed members of Local 230 of the Sign Pictorial and Display Union, Local 137 of the Sheet Metal Workers International Association, and Local 3 of the International Brotherhood of Electrical Workers. Small decals typically identified union-made electric signs in New York for a period after World War II.

A mid-sized neon shop in midcentury New York typically employed perhaps fifteen persons. Besides administrative and sales departments, the staff was divided into three main divisions: the art or layout department, where layout men designed the signs and, with the client's approval, prepared working drawings for their fabrication; the sheet metal shop, where "tin knockers" assembled metal components; and the glass department, where tube benders created the neon lamps and handled the installation of electrical components (the terms "tube bender," "glass bender," and "glass blower" are generally used interchangeably in the industry).

Layout men were typically experienced artists, sign painters, or draftsmen. Although Local 230 of the Sign Pictorial and Display Union ran a technical school for sign painters after World War II, sign designers typically learned their trade by way of apprenticeship, and they came to the job with little or no formal training. Some designers remained with the same firm for many years, lending their distinctive style to the shop's body of work; others moved from one shop to another, thus perpetuating certain visual similarities among the collective output of neon shops throughout the New York area.

Sign designs could originate with the shop's in-house layout staff or from designs provided by other designers or architects. While corporate clients typically supplied their own designs, owners of independent businesses might approach the sign shop with their own design ideas or simply leave the job to the shop's art department. Signs of the Times, the leading journal of the American sign industry from 1906 onward, frequently published illustrated articles with tips for sign designers. Pattern books such as The Electrical Advertising Sketch Portfolio by Sam Kamin (1929), and Philip DiLemme's Luminous Advertising Sketches (first released in 1935), offered model designs, much as architectural pattern books did for buildings in the previous century. While some signs (especially for large chain businesses) used standard typefaces, most used unique alphabets created by the shop's layout department. Letterforms and type designs could be sourced

ABOVE Sample designs from *Luminous Advertising Sketches* by Philip DiLemme, first published in 1935.

ABOVE The book *100 Alphabets* by Alf Becker (1940) included these sample alphabets intended for neon signs.

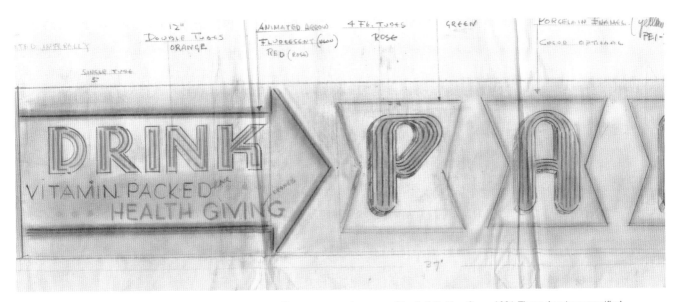

ABOVE A design drawing showing one of two fascia signs for Papaya King Inc., at Third Avenue and East 86th Street in Manhattan, prepared by Samuel Langsner of the LaSalle Sign Corp., 1964. These drawings specified colors and materials to be used in a sign's fabrication.

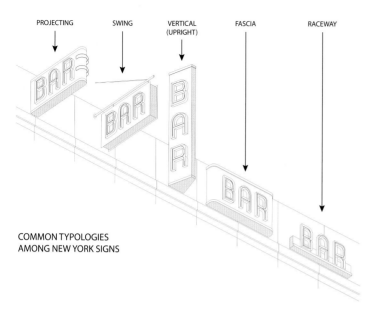

PROJECTING    SWING    VERTICAL    FASCIA    RACEWAY
                       (UPRIGHT)

COMMON TYPOLOGIES
AMONG NEW YORK SIGNS

ABOVE These five basic typologies became predominant among typical storefront signs in New York and other urban areas by the 1920s.

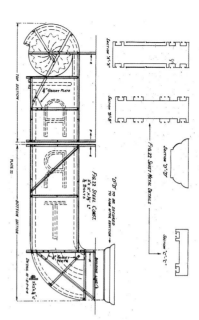

ABOVE A section drawing from Philip DiLemme's *Luminous Advertising Sketches* (1935), showing the standard sheet metal assembly of a typical neon sign.

from numerous "alphabet books" for sign painters, such as *100 Alphabets* by Alf Becker (1941), which featured adaptations of standard typefaces created by professional typographers for type foundries along with original designs of the authors. These books sometimes recommended suitable letterforms for various types of businesses. They could be reviewed with a client when working toward the final approved design.

While sign shops typically handled designs for storefront signs in-house, architects or other designers provided designs for larger or more complex installations. Artkraft Strauss, for example, fabricated many of its Times Square spectaculars from designs developed by the specialty outdoor advertising agency of Douglas Leigh. Architectural designs for cinemas and storefronts for chain businesses often included signs in their scope, thus introducing architects to neon as part of a new vocabulary of modern materials such as aluminum, porcelain enamel, glass block, stainless steel, and pigmented structural glass.

Especially after the passage of the National Housing Act in 1934, which enabled business owners to obtain government loans for capital improvements, architects deployed these modern materials in the creation of updated storefronts that soon characterized downtown commercial districts in cities and towns

across the United States. *Signs of the Times* featured New York storefront signs designed by prominent architects, including Vahan Hagopian, Horace Ginsbern, and Morris Lapidus, among others. New York's most significant surviving architect-designed neon display is the ensemble of marquees and upright signs installed at Radio City Music Hall in 1932 (see page 103).

Electric sign typologies became established by the 1910s and were carried over into the neon era essentially unchanged. Common typologies found in urban areas included "projecting," "swing," "vertical," "fascia," or "raceway" signs. "Pedestal" signs, common in New York during the gaslight era, largely disappeared by the 1920s (their cousins survive today in the form of cast-iron sidewalk clocks). The introduction of neon saw the appearance of a new type of sign, the "skeleton" sign for shop windows, which became common in the 1920s. Storefront signs typically came fitted with "flat" or "painted letters," "raised letters," or "channel letters." Larger shops such as Artkraft Strauss specialized in the construction of theater marquees and roof signs. Some shops produced quantity items (such as skeleton signs advertising various brands of beer) or generic signs sold through catalogs (such as BAR or LIQUOR STORE signs). But the bulk of the work produced in New York sign shops was custom-made in almost every detail.

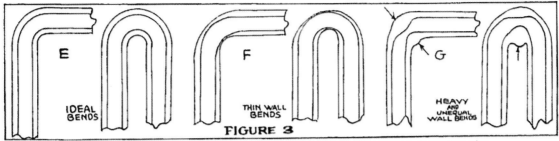

FIGURE 3

E — IDEAL BENDS    F — THIN WALL BENDS    G — HEAVY AND UNEQUAL WALL BENDS

Equal Temperature Along the Entire Length of Tube Needed to Prevent Kinks in Letter Formation

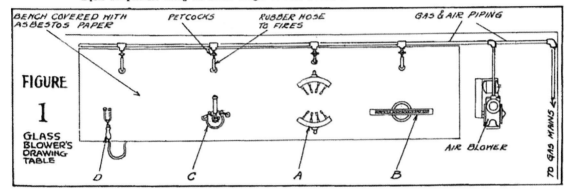

FIGURE 1

GLASS BLOWER'S DRAWING TABLE

BENCH COVERED WITH ASBESTOS PAPER — PETCOCKS — RUBBER HOSE TO FIRES — GAS & AIR PIPING — AIR BLOWER — TO GAS MAINS

D    C    A    B

ABOVE A tube bender's workbench, 1928, showing the "ribbon burner" (A), "crossfire" (B), "cannon" (C), and "hand torch" (D). This arrangement remains essentially unchanged. OPPOSITE Robbie Ingui of Artistic Neon, Inc.

at work in his shop, Ridgewood, Queens, 2010. Neon tube bending remains a highly skilled craft whose technique has changed little in the past one hundred years.

Once a design met the client's approval, the layout department prepared full-scale shop drawings for the sign's fabrication and assembly. The project then moved to the sheet metal department, where tin knockers assembled an angle-iron armature over which they affixed the sign's sheet metal exterior. The resulting sheet metal box housed any flasher mechanisms (if called for) and transformers for stepping up line voltage to the levels required for the sign's neon lamps (voltage requirements vary depending on the tube's length, diameter, and color). Many early signs featured delicate stamped zinc or copper moldings for borders or other decorative elements. These could be procured from outside firms such as Miller & Doing of Brooklyn, which offered catalogs of stock ornamental details for electric signs. Later, pared-down stainless-steel details enhanced the appearance of many signs made before the early 1950s.

With the sign's sheet metal body finished, it remained for the shop to fashion and install the neon tubes themselves. Glass bending was (and still is) a highly skilled craft, taking years to master. The earliest neon tube benders probably honed their skills by working as traditional glass blowers, perhaps specializing in

laboratory equipment, but most tube benders learned the craft by apprenticeship. At least three schools of neon glass bending operated in New York City, including the Egani Technical Institute, the Neon School of New York, and a training program offered by the International Brotherhood of Electrical Workers. These schools peaked in the late 1940s, when they enrolled veterans of World War II under the G.I. Bill.

By the 1930s, suppliers in the United States provided glass tubes in standard four-foot lengths in fixed diameters ranging from five to fifteen millimeters. For many decades, the Corning Glass Works of Corning, New York, produced most of the glass tubes used for neon signs in the United States, including a premium line made from its trademark Pyrex heat-resistant glass. Corning also supplied accessories such as electrode housings and elevation posts, which held the tubes in position. The first signs employed clear glass tubes filled with neon gas to produce its characteristic orange-red glow. Very early on, Claude and others realized that using argon instead of neon together with small amounts of mercury yielded a blue light. Colored glass tubes further extended the tube bender's palette (in addition to clear tubes, Corning's standard line

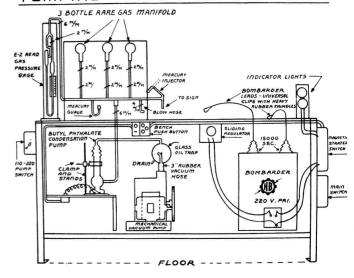

included tubes tinted blue, "noviol" gold, and "ruby red"). Finally, the introduction of tubes lined with fluorescent coatings in 1933 yielded hundreds of different colors.

The tube bender's workshop is typically centered around a broad workbench set at waist height and fitted with three specialized torches: an adjustable "ribbon burner," a "crossfire," and a "hand torch," each suited for different types of bends and shapes. With a full-scale working drawing laid across the table, a supply of four-foot tubes within reach, and a battery of torches at hand, the tube bender goes to work.

Once a length of glass is formed to the desired shape, the tube bender evacuates the tube, fills it with the specified gas, seals it, and, in a process requiring near surgical precision, connects it to two devices, usually stationed at one end of the workbench. One device, the "manifold," is joined to a tiny aperture in the glass tube, while the second—a manually regulated high-voltage transformer called a "bombarder"—is wired to the tube's electrodes. The tube bender draws air out of the tube through the manifold by activating a vacuum pump, then bombards the tube with electrical current, increasing power until an

extremely high voltage is reached. The latter process superheats the tube to free whatever impurities may remain within; these are then evacuated through a second round with the vacuum pump. Finally, by opening a stopcock on the manifold, the tube bender allows trace amounts of the specified gas (almost always neon or argon) into the tube. The stopcock is closed, the tiny opening is sealed, and the finished tube is installed on the sign.

New York sign shops typically expected their tube benders to work through sixty-five to seventy feet of neon tubing in a full day's work, or nine to ten feet per hour, depending on the nature of the shapes being produced (small letters being more labor intensive than large ones). The neon industry often relied on linear footage as a unit of measure for gauging productivity: a shop's output could be measured in terms of the number of linear feet of neon produced per week. Large Times Square spectaculars were often described in terms of the length of neon tubing used for their construction. Corning advertised that it produced "hundreds of miles" of tubing per day.

Most sign shops in New York relied on professional sign hangers to install the completed display, while permit expediters

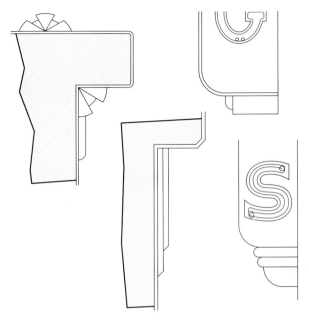

ABOVE Advertisement for stamped sheet metal moldings, 1931. Commonly used for electric signs early in the twentieth century, these moldings grew more restrained before disappearing altogether by the mid-1930s.

ABOVE Stainless-steel details typical of signs made from the mid-1930s to the early 1950s.

who specialized in outdoor signs and awnings obtained the necessary approvals from New York's Department of Buildings. Shops typically offered their customers monthly maintenance contracts to keep their displays in good working order after installation. If a length of tubing went dark, a customer with a maintenance contract simply notified the shop, which dispatched a repairman to get the display up and running again. Many neon signs remained in the care of their makers for decades after their installation.

Prevailing tastes among sign designers and their clients changed swiftly through the twentieth century, making it possible for a trained eye to deduce a sign's approximate date of fabrication based on its style and materials. In the early part of the twentieth century, electric sign shops in New York typically employed corrosion-resistant galvanized (or "galvannealed") sheet steel for most signs, which would be hand-painted by the shop's sign painters. Porcelain-enameled sheet metal provided a more durable (but more costly) alternative to galvanized steel. When specifications called for enameled steel, a sign shop typically formed the sheet metal components in-house and then sent them to an enameling plant, such as Porcelain Metals Inc., of

Long Island City, where they received a thin protective porcelain coating before being returned to the sign shop for assembly. Though it was used for electric signs as early as the first years of the twentieth century, porcelain enamel did not truly supersede painted sheet metal as the industry standard among New York sign shops until after World War II.

Stainless steel made its first appearance as an architectural metal with the construction of the Chrysler Building, completed in 1930, and it became a favored material among New York sign makers thereafter. Typically, sign designers specified porcelain enamel for the body or faces of a sign while using stainless steel for channel letters or trim. "Try to think of two sign materials that harmonize and set each other off as well as stainless steel and porcelain enamel," challenged a 1945 advertisement for the American Rolling Steel Mill Company of Pittsburgh, which marketed its products to the outdoor advertising industry through the middle decades of the twentieth century. The handsome juxtaposition of porcelain enamel and stainless steel characterized the finished appearance of typical neon signs in New York from the late 1940s through the end of the 1950s.

Sign makers began using aluminum as early as 1912, even

PAGE 31 These photographs emphasize the aesthetic of New York's midcentury neon signs, which is defined in daylight by pre-Helvetica letterforms and details executed in stainless steel and porcelain-enamel sheet metal.

ABOVE The Heinz pickle sign and the Dewey arch faced off at New York's Madison Square in 1899.

before it became common as an architectural metal. Aluminum signs grew increasingly common during the 1930s, but not until the widespread availability of competitively priced anodic coatings for architectural aluminum in the late 1950s did it displace both porcelain enamel and stainless steel to become the sign industry's sheet metal of choice by the mid-1960s, a position it still retains.

Through the 1930s electric signs in New York related stylistically to the classically inspired architecture of the same period through the use of stamped sheet metal ornament. When the popularity of a more streamlined aesthetic rendered such details out of fashion, sign makers responded by using distinctive abstract shapes for projecting signs. Through the 1940s, the work of New York sign shops remained highly influential; trade journals such as *Signs of the Times* and *Chain Store Age* featured illustrations of New York signs and storefronts that informed sign designers working in downtown areas around the world. After World War II the editors of these publications shifted the emphasis away from traditional urban centers and instead featured designs suited for roadside businesses such as motels and supermarkets, reflecting a broader trend that soon had dire consequences

for American cities large and small. While roadside signs grew increasingly flamboyant, sign shops in New York, limited partly by higher labor costs, grew more conservative in their designs during the 1950s and 1960s.

As early as the 1920s, Claude Neon and others attempted to promote neon as an architectural material for uses other than advertising signs, but with only limited success. In New York, the great neon clock of the former Williamsburgh Savings Bank tower in Brooklyn (1929) and the neon "beacon" spire of the former Cities Service tower in lower Manhattan (1932) are among the very few surviving examples of architectural neon from this period. The development of a sister technology known as "cold cathode" lighting in the late 1930s saw the closest realization of early attempts to market neon for interior lighting, but this trade lost ground to standard fluorescent lamps soon after World War II. The increased interest in neon after the late 1960s saw a revival in its use for architectural lighting in the 1970s and 1980s, but electrical advertising remained neon's primary reason for being, leaving the medium typecast in the popular consciousness for its association with commercial signs.

# A MATTER OF TASTE

⇨ Even before electric signs elicited strong feelings for and against them, civic-minded reformers sought to have outdoor advertising regulated or eliminated altogether. At their best, electric signs could be characterized, as their proponents argued, as the "art gallery of the public" or "commercially-financed light sculpture." But from the very beginning, some unscrupulous advertisers pushed the envelope beyond the pale of popular taste, giving their trade a questionable reputation with the public at large. And regardless of one's opinions toward the signs themselves, their tenacity exposed the weaknesses of high-minded civic reformers and the hypocrisy of two-talking politicians who paid lip service to the ideals of civic beautification while allowing the signs to multiply in the meantime.

Historically, various authorities made sporadic attempts to regulate outdoor signs in cities. In seventeenth-century Paris, the historian Wolfgang Schivelbusch has written, Louis XIV ordered the removal of "medieval shop signs, which projected far into the streets, obstructed the traffic and blocked the long vistas so pleasing to the Baroque, absolutist mentality." But public misgivings toward outdoor advertising did not crystallize until the nineteenth century, when commercial signs rapidly increased in number with the emergence of the modern consumer economy. For their lack of scruples, some advertisers became known as "snipers" by the 1870s and 1880s. These assailants found easy targets in prominent rock outcrops and geological formations, such as the Palisades over the Hudson River. Such abuses spurred an organized movement against outdoor advertising by the 1860s, especially in the United States and Great Britain, leading to the formation of organizations such as the British Society for Checking the Abuses of Public Advertising by 1893.

The advent of electrical advertising fanned the flames. Under the headline "Advertising Run Mad," the reformer John DeWitt Warner wrote scathingly in June 1900, "With every device of color, every possible use of light, one tradesman after another attempts to . . . force himself and his wares upon our notice." One year before, the forces on either side of this issue met head-on at New York's Madison Square. To honor Admiral Dewey's victory at the Battle of Manila Bay in 1898, a coalition of civic-minded New Yorkers hired architects McKim, Mead & White to plan the erection of a triumphal arch over the intersection of Broadway and Fifth Avenue. Immediately to the south, another landmark, the Heinz pickle sign, faced off with the Dewey arch. The stark juxtaposition between these two creations made great fodder for antisign operatives. Warner called the pickle sign "probably the most offensive advertisement that now challenges our brick-bats. . . . In the evening the dancing flash-lights of the '57 varieties' of beans, pickles, etc., thrown in the faces of all who throng Madison Square—the real center of the life and art of New York—are unimaginable except in nightmare."

Both the arch and the pickle sign disappeared within a few years, but the battle raged on. In 1910, the Municipal Art Society and other civic groups held a conference on the "electric sign nuisance," to plan "how those who have put up these signs can be forced to take them down." One speaker even questioned the signs' effectiveness for commercial purposes: "Electric signs have become so numerous, so big, and so blinding that people's attention has become deadened to them by their continual assault on the optic nerves." Antisign interests persuaded City Hall to ban overhanging electric signs along a stretch of Fifth Avenue in the mid-1910s, and the city expanded the ordinance in 1920. In 1922, the *New York Times* reported on a movement to have the ban applied to part of 42nd Street as well. But by this time, the prosign interests had also organized, forming groups such as the Master Sign Makers Association to defend against the "threatened eclipse of the midnight sun." The signs continued to shine over 42nd Street, but municipalities elsewhere enacted bans on various forms of electric signs in the years that followed.

Yet the "sign nuisance" crusade hardly represented a cross section of popular sentiment on the issue. Electric signs quickly earned a prominence in the public's understanding of the urban landscape, a position that would be acknowledged in literature, songs, and graphic art for the duration of the twentieth century. "By the 1920s photographers and painters had made electric lighting a central part of the representation of the city," the historian David Nye has written. While some decried electric signs as vulgar, others found in them an irresistible, cryptic appeal. "Fire signs announcing the night's amusements blazed on every hand," wrote Theodore Dreiser of Broadway in his novel *Sister Carrie* (1900): "All about was the night, pulsating with the thoughts of pleasure and exhilaration—the curious enthusiasm of a great city bent upon finding joy in a thousand different ways." Later, Dreiser called the "Ocean Breezes" sign at Madison Square "an inspiration and an invitation."

Similar romantic characterizations of electric signs fell in with a general artistic glorification of nocturnal imagery that intensified during the first decades of the new century. The poet Edward Sandford Martin noted in 1907 that Broadway had been "bejewled [sic] with all manner of electrical contrivance. Advertising is the motive. The result is sometimes blinding, but it is undoubtedly interesting, and, softened by due distance, it stirs the imagination and becomes even beautiful." Martin expressed a fundamentally positive appraisal of the signs: "For light itself is beautiful, and though indoors it is easy to have too much of it, out-of-doors it is hard to misuse it so extravagantly that it will not still please the eye."

Neon signs epitomized the popular image of New York as a glamorous metropolis in the 1930s. ABOVE Cover of a 1930s tourist guidebook; ABOVE RIGHT Stylized montage advertising neon products offered by the Corning Glass Works.

Artists and photographers similarly registered the growing fascination with New York's "electric landscape." The German architect Erich Mendelsohn's 1926 book *Amerika: Bilderbuch eines Architekten* (America: An Architect's Photo Album), a pictorial travelogue of the United States with photographs by the filmmaker Fritz Lang, included a double-exposed view of electric signs over Times Square. The image, blurred and skewed, suggests the signs as recalled from a dream, or perhaps in a drunken haze. Similar stylized overlay photomontages became popular among commercial and art photographers in these years to depict the dazzling effect of electric signs in New York and elsewhere. Walker Evans created a series of these images in the late 1920s, shortly after the release of Lang's film *Metropolis* (1927). Photographers such as Irving Browning, Erwin Blumenfeld, El Lissitzky, and Josef Ehm produced similar images, which appeared in advertisements for businesses such as New York Edison, as well as in illustrated guidebooks for New York and other cities.

Popular fascination with electric signs intensified with the transition to neon, which established a presence in film by the early 1930s. Some filmmakers used electric signs to convey the glamour of life in the big city, as set pieces for the extravagant Busby Berkeley–type dance numbers in films such as *42nd Street* (1933) and *Broadway Melody of 1938*. The understanding of neon as a metaphor for all things clean and modern in these years was nowhere more clearly illustrated than in a number of popular song-and-dance films of the 1930s, which juxtaposed neon illumination with equally radiant young chorus girls. Roy Roland's musical comedy *Hollywood Party* (1934) depicts a company of young female telephone operators stationed at a revolving, neonized switchboard. In the director Ray Enright's film *Dames* of the same year, pretty young showgirls make themselves even prettier before an array of neon-framed mirrors.

Neon played its greatest role in the director Mervyn LeRoy's film *Gold Diggers of 1933*. In a lavish dance number choreographed by Busby Berkeley, twirling chorus girls brandishing neon violins serenade a pair of young lovers portrayed by Dick Powell and Ruby Keeler, to the lilting melody of *The Shadow Waltz*. That same year more than 40,000 feet of neon tubing illuminated pavilions at Chicago's Century of Progress exposition, which also featured glass-bending demonstrations in a special exhibit devoted to the manufacture of neon signs. Neon had reached its zenith, but it wouldn't last long.

By the 1940s, the nighttime neon conveyed something more sinister. Electric signs, especially obsolete ones, hung over the doors or flashed through the windows of nearly every seedy bar and run-down flophouse depicted onscreen. A defective sign

As neon's reputation suffered after World War II, signmakers found an untarnished alternative in fluorescent lamps, introduced by General Electric in 1938. ABOVE The cover to the 1949 edition of The Neon Wilderness, by Nelson Algren; ABOVE RIGHT Early GE promotional material for fluorescent lamps.

made the scene more evocative: lights partially dimmed or visibly and audibly flickering. Early on, incandescent bulb signs set the tone best. The incandescent sign depicted in Edward Hopper's painting Chop Suey (1929) suggests something worn and obsolete, depicted at a time when bulb signs were rapidly yielding to neon. H. Bruce Humberstone's 1941 film I Wake Up Screaming portrayed its menaced protagonists (Betty Grable and Victor Mature) rendezvousing at an all-night "adults only" movie house whose incandescent marquee seems forgotten by time.

After World War II, artists, writers, and filmmakers seized on neon signs to convey the unwholesome air that obsolete incandescent bulb signs suggested in the previous decade. Neon's genre-defining association with film noir can be traced to what may be the very first English-language use of the term: "In a walk-up room, filled with the intermittent flashing of a neon sign from across the street, a man is waiting to murder or be murdered . . . the specific ambience of film noir, a world of darkness and violence, with a central figure whose motives are usually greed, lust and ambition, whose world is filled with fear, reached its fullest realization in the Forties," wrote Charles Higham and Joel Greenberg in 1968. The films both reflected and reinforced the evolving popular understanding of neon signs in the built environment.

In 1944, Dick Powell and neon light crossed paths again in the film Murder, My Sweet, which was the director Edward Dmytryk's screen adaptation of Raymond Chandler's novel Farewell, My Lovely (1940). In the first minutes of the film, a flickering neon sign sets a disquieting tone: "The joint looked like trouble," explains Powell's voiceover. It's A Wonderful Life, Frank Capra's perennial Christmas stalwart of 1946, ushered neon further into the realm of ill repute. The selfless protagonist George Bailey (James Stewart) is let loose in a grotesque alternate reality of what his hometown would be like had he never been born. Where a sedate wooden placard once welcomed visitors to Bedford Falls, George is unnerved to find a crass neon sign marking the entrance to Pottersville. Later, Bailey stumbles horror-struck down snow-covered streets, confronted by glaring neon signs over taxi-dance halls and burlesque houses. Neon became the agent of big city immorality infiltrating the picket-fence towns of fine upstanding Americans.

Other films emphasized a parallel between neon signs and various idioms of urban vice, particularly alcohol, an association not without basis. "With the repeal of Prohibition," noted the authors of a short history of neon signs in 1935, the neon business "received a definite advance. Old and new breweries and liquor distributors decided almost to a man on the neon sign as one of their major

ABOVE A Times Square "taxi dance" hall, c. 1939. Neon signs became increasingly associated with unseemly, midway-type enterprises by the 1940s. ABOVE RIGHT Guilt by association: the outdoor advertising industry's "worst elements" perpetuated popular misgivings toward outdoor advertising that

came to a head with the passage of the federal Highway Beautification Act in 1965. OPPOSITE Gotham City Video, 687 Eighth Avenue near Times Square. Signs like these once perpetuated popular misgivings toward neon signs generally, but are now viewed by many with a nostalgic affection.

advertising mediums." John Farrow's 1948 noir thriller *The Big Clock* shows its main character, a successful New York magazine editor (Ray Milland), off on a bender. Neon signs flash the names of bar after bar as corks pop and martini glasses clink in the background, in what became a standard lap-fade sequence that evoked earlier photomontages by Walker Evans and others. The 1962 film *Days of Wine and Roses* ends with recovering alcoholic Joe Clay (Jack Lemmon) gazing out into the night, transfixed by the sight of a sign blinking the word *BAR* into the darkness as the screen fades to black.

Works of literature in this period similarly echoed neon's fall from grace. With the decline of America's urban centers, inner-city neon seemed best suited to cast its glow over faded skid row bars and flophouses and the unsavory characters who frequented them. In *The Neon Wilderness* (1947), a collection of short stories set mainly in Chicago, Nelson Algren introduced his readers to "life in the raw . . . love with the lace torn off and its skirts dragging in the gutters." His characters inhabited a neon-lit world of darkness and violence: "This was the true jungle, the neon wilderness. Sometimes the dull red lights, off and on, off and on, made the spilled beer along the floor appear like darkly flowing blood."

Neon also lit the world inhabited by fringe characters like

Sal Paradise, Jack Kerouac's alter ego in his semiautobiographical Beat novel *On the Road*, written in the early 1950s and published in 1957. "Right across the street there was trouble," Paradise recounts: "An old rickety rundown rooming house was the scene of some kind of tragedy. . . . Sobbings came from within. I could hear everything, together with the hum of my hotel neon. I never felt sadder in my life." Neon signs appear repeatedly in *City of Night* (1963), John Rechy's autobiographical novel of a young male hustler's itinerant journey across the United States. "Along that strip," he wrote of downtown Los Angeles circa 1960, "the gray hotels welcome the scores and malehustlers: No Questions Asked. For a few minutes—unless you haven't got another place . . . you occupy the fleetingly rented room, where inevitably a neonlight outside will wink off and on feebly."

Meanwhile, outside the nation's fading downtowns, new neon signs enjoyed a separate identity free of associations with noirish vice and urban decay. In the postwar years, neon came to be identified as much with Route 66, Las Vegas, and the suburban commercial strip as with the Great White Way or the traditional urban streetscape. By the 1960s, however, these images, too, carried a dark side as a revived sign-nuisance movement set its

sights on "highway beautification." For an idealistic generation of young writers and artists, neon symbolized a materialistic society in the grip of corporate commodity pushers indifferent to the social ills around them. Probably no one expressed this notion more piquantly than Paul Simon in "The Sounds of Silence," first released in 1964, which described a world whose people prayed to a "neon God," where flashing neon signs "stabbed the eyes" of those seeking quiet contemplation.

The precipitous decline of Times Square in the 1960s and 1970s linked neon with graphic forms of immorality that would have scandalized even the most debauched degenerates of Pottersville a generation before. As the area's burlesque houses and amusement arcades devolved into porno palaces and adult bookstores, neon remained the square's favored form of advertising, its vivid glow apparently communicating on the same wavelength as the basest human instincts. The first edition of *City of Night* featured an image of "the deuce," the block of West 42nd Street immediately west of Times Square, on its dust jacket. Rechy's description of Times Square anticipated the grotesque scenes for which the area later became known in films such as John Schlesinger's *Midnight Cowboy* of 1969: "Giant signs—Bigger! Than! Life!—blink off and on. And a great hungry sign groping luridly at the darkness screams: F * A * S * C * I * N * A * T * I * O * N . . . like a possessive lover—or like a powerful drug—it lured me. FASCINATION! I stopped working. . . . And I returned, dazzled, to this street."

By the following decade, the grit-covered neon tubes trailing off into the distance through the rear window of Travis Bickle's Checker cab in the Martin Scorsese film *Taxi Driver* (1976) symbolized the sordid underworld of a debased city. In the director William Friedkin's film *Cruising* (1980), the neon sign over the entrance of Times Square's St. James Hotel portends the brutal slaying about to take place in a cheap room upstairs. Scorsese and other young filmmakers in this period used old neon signs as metaphors for their world-weary characters and the gritty demimonde they inhabited. The signs featured in these films convey a sense of the rampant disillusionment that grew in the Vietnam era: with their upbeat scripts and cheerful colors naively shining out into the darkness, they sounded an elegy for the lost optimism of an earlier time. Movie house marquees on 42nd Street advertised explicit porno films screening in old theaters with names like "Victory," "Lyric," "Liberty," and "Empire." No one could ignore the irony.

ABOVE Though it was often associated with less wholesome trades, neon advertised all sorts of businesses, as these old New York signs still affirm.

# NEAR-DEATH EXPERIENCE

⇨ By the late 1960s, sign shops moved away from neon for new technologies and materials that changed the character of modern illuminated signs. Acrylic-panel signs and vinyl awnings lit from within by off-the-shelf fluorescent tubes became standard storefront advertising throughout New York. Not only were these signs less expensive to manufacture and maintain, but they had the virtue of being completely divorced from neon's tarnished repute. The increased use of standard typefaces, especially Helvetica (introduced in 1957), and a mass trend toward modernized corporate logos by designers such as Saul Bass further widened the aesthetic gap. Neon signs that continued to be produced generally assumed a new character, with their glass tubes concealed behind colored plastic lenses.

The technologies that superseded neon in the 1960s made their debut in the 1930s, and their rise to prominence coincided with and helped facilitate neon's declining image in the midcentury decades. Ironically, while the first neon signs were often installed for chain stores and large corporations, corporate retailers were the first to abandon neon for new shadow-box signs made from modern materials that eventually redefined America's commercial landscape.

In 1938, Goodyear Tires unveiled a new standard-issue outdoor sign for its dealerships nationwide. "This means turning away from luminous-tubing displays," reported *Signs of the Times*. Goodyear's standard neon signs were to be replaced by internally lit shadow-box signs. "Twelve years ago . . . a red neon sign was a novelty. In most cities there were only a few such signs, and therefore their attraction value was immense. Of recent years, however, the streets of every city and town have been lined with red neon signs until today they are virtually 'rivers of red,' according to Goodyear, and the signs have lost their individual character." Goodyear found other problems with neon, too. "Neon tubing on the face of a sign has a tendency to make the lettering hard to read during the daytime and it collects dirt and grime, making an ugly appearance," explained a company spokesperson. The new signs, furthermore, would require "no costly maintenance; no tubing, transformers, or wiring to replace."

In the same year, General Electric introduced the fluorescent "lumiline" tube lamp. Available in standard sizes, these combined the off-the-shelf practicality of incandescent bulbs with the low-energy consumption of neon tubes. Largely excluded from the

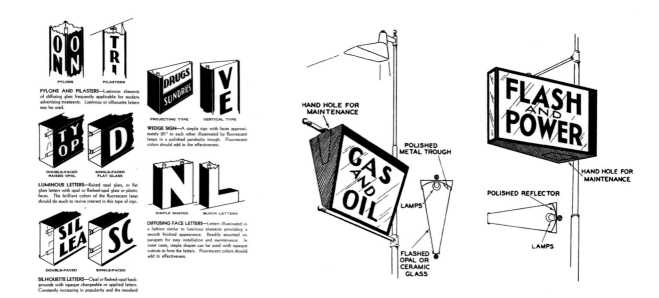

ABOVE General Electric provided sketches and technical data to encourage the use of fluorescent lamps in outdoor advertising.

neon industry after it declined to purchase Claude's patents, General Electric promoted internally lit shadow-box signs for outdoor advertising as an alternative to neon throughout the 1920s and 1930s, but with little success. With the introduction of fluorescent lamps, the company redoubled its efforts in 1938, providing sketches, technical data, and field representatives to encourage the use of fluorescent lamps in outdoor advertising. New York sign shops began installing fluorescent lamp signs by the time of the 1939 World's Fair.

General Electric's promotional literature initially showed fluorescent lamps encased within sign faces of "flashed opal and ceramic glass." But very shortly, another new technology emerged that gave the shadow-box sign an even greater edge. The Philadelphia-based plastics company Rohm & Haas introduced a new acrylic resin plastic, marketed as Plexiglas, in 1936, and began aggressively promoting its use for electric signs soon afterward. Acrylic resin plastic, Rohm & Haas advised sign makers in 1939, "glitters like crystal, and it conducts light around curves. It can be bent and twisted without breaking. It is not brittle, it softens under heat and can be shaped when hot. It is only 45 percent as heavy as ordinary glass. It is so strong that it will withstand a hard blow without breaking and it is as hard as copper." Best of all, the

company explained, "Fluorescent tube lighting is especially suitable for use with acrylic sheets."

The marriage of fluorescent lamps and acrylic resin plastics took place at the 1939 New York World's Fair. Whereas neon had been a key attraction of the 1933 Chicago fair, the planners of the 1939 World's Fair kept neon tubes out of sight. "The designers of the New York fair . . . introduced restrictions as to both signs and lighting that were intended to prevent clashing of colors or garish effects in the exhibit area," reported *Signs of the Times*. "In general, no exterior sign could show exposed tubing and all lighting would have to meet the requirements of the fair's board of design." While neon was not altogether banished, the real darling of the occasion was the new fluorescent lamp. And, per the requirements of the fair's planners, most neon signs installed there had their tubes concealed behind reversed metal channels or translucent acrylic lenses.

Electric sign development came to a standstill during World War II, but in the postwar years, the new look in electric signs demonstrated at the 1939 fair gradually rose to the fore. The change came incrementally. Neon managed to hold its own through the 1950s, and indeed these proved some of its best years. But in the following decade, as nationwide chains and franchise

ABOVE. A typical mid-1960s fluorescent-lit acrylic panel sign at The Pizza Wagon, 8610 Fifth Avenue, Brooklyn. By the late 1960s, sign shops moved away from neon in favor of internally lit acrylic panel signs.

businesses adopted new standardized fluorescent-lit acrylic-panel signs, the previous generation of exposed-tube neon signs came to be seen as decidedly passé.

At first, popular sentiment extended little sympathy toward old neon signs. In *God's Own Junkyard*, the architect and critic Peter Blake decried downtown corridors bedraggled with decades' accretions of projecting signs, juxtaposing illustrations of Canal Street in New Orleans (bad) against the Lawn at Thomas Jefferson's University of Virginia (good). The sign industry, in a moment of introspection brought on by the enactment of the federal Highway Beautification Act in October 1965, took Blake's message to heart. In 1966, the National Electric Sign Association (NESA) launched a series of "Scrap Old Signs" programs across the United States. "The S.O.S. program resulted in the removal of a large number of obsolete and unsightly signs," said the association. Scarcely four decades after its introduction, the neon sign hit rock bottom.

## SYMPATHY FOR THE DEVIL

➡ At the very moment when neon seemed near its demise, a groundswell of enthusiasm for luminous tubes and for the old signs themselves began to gain momentum. "There are several indications [in New York], and perhaps in other cities as well, that neon is on its way back," wrote a contributor to *Signs of the Times* in 1966. The story cited an offshoot of the pop art movement that had adopted neon tubes as a new medium. "Neon is the purest, hippest color in the world," said the artist Billy Apple in a story published in *Time* the following month.

In fact, neon never entirely lost its appeal to many artists and writers. "Neon in daylight is a great pleasure," wrote Frank O'Hara in 1956. Though unflattering depictions of neon signs in mid-century film and literature did much to undermine the signs' mainstream appeal, such portrayals (particularly in the context of Beat novels such as *On the Road*) together with the dissociation of old signs from the increasingly negative image of "corporate America" set the stage for the latter-day appreciation of neon signs by lending them a bohemian, "road-culture" mystique after the late 1960s.

ABOVE Philippe Wine & Liquor, 212 West 23rd Street, Manhattan. After the 1960s, new storefront signs characterized by fluorescent illumination, acrylic plastic sign faces and standard typefaces such as Helvetica made a stark contrast against the previous generation of exposed tube neon signs.

Artists such as the Czech sculptor Dietmar Elger had worked with neon tubes as early as the 1930s. More neon sculpture appeared after World War II, including works by the Italian artist Lucio Fontana in the early 1950s, and later pieces by artists such as Chryssa and Mario Merz. Still, neon art struggled to find its niche until the ascendance of pop art in the 1960s, a movement that appropriated images and materials associated with consumer culture for use in unexpected contexts. The appearance of landmark works by artists such as Bruce Nauman and Richard Serra established neon as a legitimate medium by the mid-1960s.

At the same time, a generation of young architects began to reexamine the notion of clutter in the built environment. "Architects . . . do not easily acknowledge the validity of the commercial vernacular," wrote Robert Venturi, Denise Scott Brown, and Steven Izenour in *Learning from Las Vegas* (1972). In the wake of *God's Own Junkyard* and the Highway Beautification Act, these architects wrote of "the deadness that results from too great a preoccupation with tastefulness and total design."

Within a few years, the distinction between contemporary electric signs and their neon predecessors widened to a point where the old signs could be seen with a nostalgic affection as objects of vernacular Americana, or works of commercial folk art. "Save those old neon signs!" advised *Signs of the Times* in a 1974 story: "There's more value in many of them than the junk dealer will offer." The story featured a combined neon shop and art gallery called Let There Be Neon, co-founded two years earlier by the New York multimedia artist Rudi Stern in the formerly industrial part of Manhattan known as SoHo. Old neon signs soon appeared in the collections of cultural institutions such as the Smithsonian National Museum of American History and the Henry Ford Museum.

In 1977, enthusiasts of neon signs and related relics organized to form the Society for Commercial Archeology, dedicated to "documentation, education, advocacy and conservation to encourage public awareness and understanding of these significant elements of our heritage." The society's mission bore fruit with the publication of books such as Warren Belasco's *Americans on the Road* (1979), *California Crazy* by Jim Heimann (1980), *End of the Road* by John Margolies (1981), and *Main Street to Miracle Mile* by Chester Liebs (1985). By the late 1970s, the same "junkyard" decried by Peter Blake as an "interminable wasteland" of "billboards, jazzed-up diners, used-car lots, drive-in movies, beflagged gas stations, and garish motels" had become a treasure trove of "roadside Americana." Neon lit the way.

ABOVE LEDs have succeeded neon and fluorescent lamps as a novel source of artificial illumination with incredible versatility. Concealed beneath acrylic lenses, LEDs have taken the place of neon in modern storefront signs.

# THE LED REVOLUTION

⇨ The revived interest in neon sustained luminous tubes as a commercial and artistic medium through the end of the twentieth century. But the emergence of practical light emitting diodes (LEDs) for outdoor advertising in the twenty-first century presented a new challenge. First introduced in the early 1960s, LEDs became common as indicator lights on solid-state electronic appliances through the 1970s and 1980s. By the early years of the new century, they advanced to a state of practicality that has made them the most versatile artificial light source in history, appearing everywhere from traffic lights to children's sneakers. In New York, LEDs can be found in nightclubs and subway cars and, since 2007, on the Christmas tree at Rockefeller Center.

A 2011 survey by *Signs of the Times* found that neon had lost considerable ground to LEDs in recent years: "As expected, the change from 2007 to 2010 is dramatic. Whereas neon had still dominated LEDs (33.3% to 23.4%) then, LEDs now more than double the use of neon (40.1% to 17.9%)." Masked behind acrylic lenses, LEDs have taken the place of neon with almost no visible impact on the design of typical contemporary storefront signs. Neon tubes have almost completely disappeared from Times Square, as flood-lit billboards and sculpted LED jumbotrons are now advertisers' favored medium. LEDs have even moved in on neon skeleton signs, though many of these have been carefully disguised to look as much as possible like their neon predecessors.

While neon will likely live on as a specialty item for its sheer charisma, the disappearance of neon signs old and new in recent years has engendered a renewed appreciation for them, fueled by the urgency to document a craft and an aesthetic that seems increasingly endangered. In New York, the emergence of LED illumination has coincided with an onslaught of new development that has lent old neon signs an added significance for many who identify the signs with old neighborhood institutions and other fragile things whose place in the city has come into question amid surging demand for real estate.

# VITAL SIGNS

⇨ In 1980 an old cafeteria near the World Trade Center reopened as a fashionable French bistro. "The warehouse district of Lower Manhattan is not the place one would expect to find French food, or indeed any first-class cooking, but the Odeon, a former cafeteria

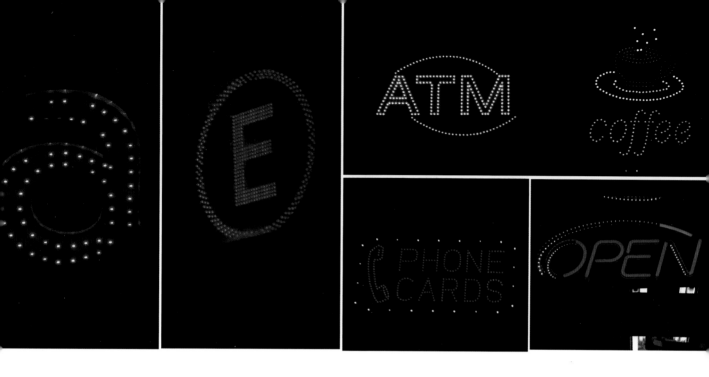

on West Broadway at Thomas Street, serves fine nouvelle cuisine," reported the *New York Times* that November. "The warehouse-lined streets are no longer totally dark and empty at night. The gaunt buildings are rapidly being converted to lofts, restaurants and shops." Rather than gut the space, the restaurateur Keith McNally kept the former cafeteria largely as he found it, right down to its old neon sign outside (see pages 96–97). This marked a bellwether for a revival in which neon signs and other objects formerly associated with urban decline began to assume new appeal amid a revived demand for urban real estate.

In the years that followed, this revival grew to endanger the very relics—old cafeterias, neon signs, and so on—celebrated at places like the Odeon. By the early 1980s, the proposed redevelopment of Times Square induced an organized resistance to a plan that threatened to oversanitize the area. Before the decade was out, eulogies for mom-and-pop stores displaced by corporate retailers and upscale restaurants became commonplace in neighborhoods such as Manhattan's Upper West Side. As the city's revival reached a fever pitch in the years leading to the financial crisis of 2008, a growing number of New Yorkers voiced dissatisfaction with the wave of revitalization that some felt had overcorrected for the city's previous period of stagnation. For

their association with old independent businesses, neon signs of a certain vintage had come to symbolize a sense of character and identity that has been displaced from much of the city since the 1980s.

The revived enthusiasm for neon signs went beyond humble storefront displays. In 1992, the removal of the giant roof sign from the former headquarters of Pan American World Airways prompted a small outcry, even though the building's new owner, the Metropolitan Life Insurance Company, planned to install a similar display in its place. The original sign had elicited less favorable commentary when it first appeared three decades earlier. "One of the tallest, most prominently situated skyscrapers in the world . . . is now crowned with the cryptic, mammoth words 'PAN AM,'" wrote Peter Blake in *God's Own Junkyard*: "Like children, we insist upon labeling most of our buildings, putting the name of the owner or tenant up on top in giant letters." Somehow, the Pan Am sign won admirers over the years. "Couldn't they just leave the sign up and take the building down?" asked the architect Robert A. M. Stern of the big neon letters over Park Avenue in 1992.

The Pan Am sign wouldn't be so lucky, but other signs have indeed outlived the buildings that once supported them. In the 1980s, Jersey City's famous "Colgate Clock" spectacular survived

ABOVE Hi-Life Bar, Columbus Avenue, Manhattan, with signs by Tee-Pee neon, 1992. With originals in short supply, some businesses have installed new signs styled after old ones.

the demolition of the company's waterfront factory complex and remains in place today. Two decades later, developers in Long Island City re-erected an eighty-year-old Pepsi-Cola spectacular when the plant on which it stood made way for new waterfront apartment towers (see page 168). In nearby Williamsburg, another developer proposed the preservation of a similar waterfront sign that advertises Domino Sugar, though the building to which it is affixed—a twentieth-century addition to the historic sugar refinery next door—was slated for demolition.

In commenting on the disappearance of the Pan Am sign, the architecture critic Paul Goldberger rationalized the affection for relic signs by citing the expiration of their commercial role: "Once Pan Am had gone out of business no one could challenge the fact that the sign was a historical artifact, not a piece of advertising." But other indications suggest that the appeal of many signs is indeed spurred on by lingering associations with their commercial origins. In 1983, many New Yorkers voiced concern that the proposed Times Square cleanup threatened to eliminate the square's characteristic neon spectaculars. The Municipal Art Society spearheaded a plea to keep the signs, though this same organization had led the charge *against* electric signs in the early years of the twentieth century. "Signs in Times Square are like

redwoods in California," explained Kent Barwick, then MAS's president. "They have to be protected." In 1987, the city enacted new zoning *requiring* the installation of electric signs in and around Times Square.

Elsewhere, New York's Landmarks Preservation Commission has acted to preserve some historic signs. Though the commission has yet to extend protection to any sign in its own right (other cities have done this), it regulates the fate of signs that are part of designated properties. The commission unanimously rejected the proposed removal of a long-dark neon sign proclaiming the words TUDOR CITY from the roof of the historic apartment complex in 1995 (see pages 120–121). Elsewhere, it has required the restoration or replication of signs such as the neon marquees of the Apollo (page 51) and New Amsterdam (page 92) theaters, and it has vetted proposals to re-letter existing roof signs, such as that atop the former Guardian Life building at Union Square. Other roof signs, such as those of the New Yorker Hotel in midtown and Lackawanna Terminal in Hoboken, have been restored voluntarily (though both signs now employ LEDs rather than neon tubes).

Yet despite repeated episodes suggesting the potential of commercial landmarks to become valued parts of the cityscape, electric signs both old and new face opposition from different

ABOVE This neon sign had hung over the door of McHale's Bar and Grill on Eighth Avenue and is now displayed in Emmett O'Lunney's Irish Pub near Times Square.

entities dedicated to improving New York's quality of life. Outside Times Square, zoning ordinances preclude the installation of new roof signs like Long Island City's Pepsi spectacular. Meanwhile, the nostalgic sentiment that so adores historic neon signs is fundamentally antithetical to the forces of progress that brought these signs into being in the first place. And perhaps most ironically, the recent hyperactivity of those same market forces has profoundly endangered all things ephemeral in the urban landscape in Manhattan and other parts of the city.

New York's zoning ordinances have all but erased illuminated roof signs from the city's skyline (a grandfather clause allows the installation of new electric roof signs where such displays have existed continuously since before the ordinance went into effect). Such policy reflects age-old misgivings toward outdoor advertising that live on into the twenty-first century. In 1986, Paul Goldberger decried a new roof sign advertising Hitachi electronics at Columbus Circle as "one of the sharpest visual intrusions the midtown skyline has seen in years," though old photographs by Walker Evans and Berenice Abbott show some of New York's most extravagant spectaculars at the same location in years past. Farther downtown, the illumination of a giant neon umbrella advertising the Traveler's Group insurance company stirred the ire of its neighbors in 1998.

"We wish we could shoot the stupid thing down altogether," remarked a member of the TriBeCa Community Association, which successfully negotiated to have the sign dimmed during the evening hours (the sign, which had slipped through a loophole in the city's zoning and building codes, has since been removed).

Other cities and towns maintain ordinances that outlaw the creation of signs like those now on display at the Smithsonian Institution. The historic village of Rhinebeck in upstate New York boasts old neon signs over the entrances of Foster's Coach House Tavern and the Northern Dutchess Pharmacy that could not be installed under current zoning codes. Officials in Chatham Borough, New Jersey, "prodded by complaints from historic preservationists and others," banned neon signs there in 1995. In 2010, officials in Nyack, New York, insisted that a proposed Walgreen's drugstore reduce its signage, which they called "obnoxious, offensive and out of context," though the project location stood on a four-lane highway by exit ramps serving the New York State Thruway. At the very same moment, preservationists in New Orleans rallied to protect a historic four-story neon extravaganza marking the spot of another Walgreen's, located on the same stretch of Canal Street cited contemptuously by Peter Blake as a case study in clutter in the 1960s.

J. Crew Men's Shop, 237 West Broadway, Manhattan, formerly Hecht's Liquor Store. In gentrifying neighborhoods, upscale businesses have retained old neon signs over their storefronts even when the sign has nothing to do with their trade.

Meanwhile, back in New York, old neon signs have become poster children for a movement repulsed by the relentless pace of change sweeping the city. A small handful of more fortunate old signs have benefited from their newfound mystique: some are restored or replicated. Elsewhere, a handful of new shops and restaurants have kept old neon signs hanging over their doors even if the sign has nothing do with the business within. More commonly, signs retired from active duty are moved indoors as objects of décor.

Still, the preservation of a few old signs is a small, at times superficial gesture toward what many feel is being lost along with those that disappear. The fashionable businesses that are most inclined to preserve vintage signs are often the same kinds of places maligned for bringing about rent hikes that drive out the old shops that put these signs up originally. The ongoing debate over the changing face of the city has become a definitive theme of contemporary New York. Prominent writers have lent their voices to a chorus of sometimes impassioned overtures lamenting not only the loss of affordable housing, independent bookshops, revival movie theaters, old watering holes, and mom-and-pop corner stores, but also of the graffiti and grit that conventional wisdom once identified with the demise of urban life in America. A

November 2010 survey conducted by the Internet blog gothamist. com asking readers "Which Times Square Do You Prefer?" found that two-thirds of respondents favored "The gritty one, Pre-Disneyfication" over "The current one, Olive Garden 4-ever!"

Neon signs figure prominently in this discussion. A blog entitled "Lost City," chronicling the disappearance of "vestiges of Old New York as they are steamrolled under or threatened by the currently ruthless real estate market and the City Fathers' disregard for Gotham's historical and cultural fabric," featured on its masthead a photograph of the neon sign that formerly hung over McHale's, an old Hell's Kitchen bar and grill shuttered in December 2005. The epitaph reads: "The late, great McHale's, the death of which inspired the birth of this blog." (The sign later turned up as décor in an Irish bar nearby). Neon likewise appears throughout the book *Storefront*, a photographic homage to various forms of independently run businesses. "Astoundingly, almost one-third of the stores pictured here have disappeared," wrote the authors James and Karla Murray in 2008 (more have closed since then). "We happened to witness first hand the alarming rate at which the shops were disappearing, and decided to preserve what we could of what remained."

Yet in their day, these same neon signs were identified with

For its sheer charisma, neon will likely live on as a specialty item. ABOVE LEFT St. Mark's Bookshop, 31 Third Avenue, Manhattan, sign by Barter Signs, c. 1993.

ABOVE RIGHT A recent neon installation at American Apparel, East Houston Street, Manhattan.

the forces of change that bring about their demise today. In his 1939 essay "Obituary of a Gin Mill," the *New Yorker* columnist Joseph Mitchell expressed his dismay over the sudden makeover of Dick's Bar, one of his favorite dives. "Dick's old place was dirty and it smelled like the zoo, but it was genuine." Mitchell decried Dick's new incarnation as "a big, classy place with a chromium and glass-brick front, a neon sign in four colors, a mahogany bar, a row of chromium bar stools with red-leather seats like those in the uptown cocktail lounges." At around the same time, the writer Charles Green Shaw wandered the city seeking out odd relics for a book called *New York, Oddly Enough*, published in 1938. Among Shaw's favorite urban artifacts, old wooden "trade signs" ranked highly: "They are of a day prior to the advent of skyscrapers, motorcars, or subways. Nevertheless, quite without the enticement of neon gas or electric illumination, they continue to perform their function precisely as they did in days of yore."

To be sure, the disappearance of old neon signs throughout New York is a potent visual barometer of the city's most recent metamorphosis. Still, as sweeping as New York's recent period of change has been, one can easily delineate any number of narrow chronological windows in its history during which the city experienced more extreme degrees of physical change. "A man born in New York forty years ago finds nothing, absolutely nothing, of the New York he knew," a contributor to *Harper's New Monthly Magazine* noted in 1856. Theodore Dreiser published *The Color of the Great City*, a collection of essays on New York, largely because he realized "how swiftly and steadily the city was changing and old landmarks and conditions were being done away with." The year was 1923. New York, he wrote, had grown "duller because less differentiated."

At around the same time, the advent of high-rise construction paved the way for a building boom that prompted the passage of the city's 1916 Zoning Resolution to regulate new construction throughout the five boroughs. Newly completed elevated subway lines coursed over unpaved roads and old farms in parts of upper Manhattan and Jackson Heights, Queens, where vast swaths of dense urban development took shape within a few years. After World War II, urban renewal programs administered under Robert Moses saw entire neighborhoods taken off the map. The pace of change in the postwar years galvanized staunch opposition, personified by the writer and activist Jane Jacobs, and in 1966 it led to the creation of a new city agency—the Landmarks Preservation Commission—charged with protecting the city's most important works of architecture in perpetuity.

The change that has swept the city since the 1980s came on the heels of a prolonged period of stagnation that allowed for the accretion of relics (old neon signs and others) that might have vanished long ago had New York's economy continued to grow unabated. "Our city is molting," *New York* magazine's architecture critic wrote in 2008, noting that the city's Department of Buildings authorized the construction of more than 77,000 new buildings (and issued some 44,000 demolition permits) over the previous fifteen years. By mourning the loss of these old signs and their associated businesses without pausing to consider the merits of their successors, critics of the changing city sometimes overlook the fact that these signs are products of the same forces of change that reshape the city now. The old signs stand out today because they represent scarce fragments of a diminished whole: of thousands that once existed, only a few remain. In this sense, their appeal relies on a process that has destroyed the better part of the whole.

Yet, by the same token, the widespread appreciation for these signs today indicates that such relics possess a unique ability to enhance the quality of the built environment, even if only in numbers small enough to allow the ongoing change that is essential to a city's vitality. It is this contrast between new and old within a framework of continual change that gives meaning to the "authenticity" of the objects and institutions that surround us. In New York's fast changing landscape, the old signs are more than objects of nostalgic sentiment: they stand for the importance of maintaining a balance between the offbeat and the mainstream.

Throughout the history of neon signs, attitudes toward them have reflected undercurrents shaping the built environment at large. The intensified appreciation for these signs in New York today reveals not just a nostalgic longing for the past, the fact that vinyl awnings make for less interesting street furniture, or that the powers governing the city's ongoing development have yet to acknowledge the value of a certain degree of clutter in the landscape: it reveals the elusiveness of an ideal balance between opposing forces of progress and stagnation that have left the old signs in their wake. The problem is not that New York is changing: New York is a city wrought of change. It is that the city is losing its habitat for the organic survival of places, artifacts, and people that are outside the mainstream. For as much as progress and innovation are fundamental to New York's ability to stay relevant both economically and culturally in a changing world, so, too, are subcultures whose existence in various forms throughout history has been a fundamental part of what makes a city a desirable place in which to live.

AMERICAN LEGION

金玉珠寶銀行
GOLDEN JADE JEWELRY INC.

THE SIGNS

# MANHATTAN

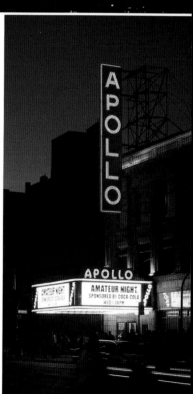

## LT. B.R. KIMLAU AMERICAN LEGION POST 1291

191 Canal Street,
c. 1959*

This sign overlooking Canal Street in Chinatown testifies for the popularity of extended (horizontally elongated) letterforms in the 1950s and 60s. "The present trend in extended type design seems undiminishing," wrote J.I. Biegeleisen in the *Book of 100 Typeface Alphabets*, published in 1965: "Pick up and examine any of the smartly designed magazine and newspaper ads and you will see the popularity of wide or extended types in use today."

## ANGELO'S OF MULBERRY STREET

146 Mulberry Street,
c. 1955, union sign shop no.19

Though Little Italy seems to get littler every year, Mulberry Street still boasts a handful of Italian-American businesses whose old neon signs attest to their longevity. Angelo's opened in 1902. Its sign makes a brief cameo in Martin Scorsese's 1973 film *Mean Streets*. The icey hue of its neon script goes well with the stainless steel sheet metal behind.

## APOLLO THEATRE

253 West 125th Street,
1940 (facsimile by North Shore Neon, 2006)

Built in 1914 as Hurtig & Seamon's New Burlesque Theatre, the Apollo's real significance derives from its emergence in the 1930s as one of the first major theaters in the United States to welcome black performers and audiences. The theater originally installed its streamlined, neon-lit marquee and vertical sign in 1940, replacing an earlier, highly eccentric incandescent display. When the Apollo underwent comprehensive restoration work in 2006, its management commissioned the North Shore Neon Sign Co. of Deer Park, Long Island to install a convincing facsimile of the 1940 signage, though LED panels replaced its silhouette letter marquee.

NOTE
* indicates an unconfirmed date suggested by records at New York City Department of Buildings

? indicates an unconfirmed maker

⇧

## ARTHUR'S TAVERN

Grove Street, 1938 (fascia);
c.1950* (vertical)

Arthur Raganati opened this tavern on the ground floor of an old Greenwich Village rowhouse in 1937 and the following year installed the neon fascia sign that still shines over its door. The vertical sign above it came later. (The sign glows white today, but has a pinkish hue over Jack Kerouac's shoulder in a well known photograph of the Beat writer taken in the 1950s.) Next door, the fascia sign of Marie's Crisis Café dates to 1936.

⇧

## BACK FENCE
155 Bleecker Street, 1946

Fluorescent neon in four colors wraps the corner of this ancient Greenwich Village townhouse that the Back Fence has called home since 1946. Adjacent pink and reddish luminous hues illustrate the difference between tubes lined in fluorescent coatings (pink) and pure neon red in clear glass tubes.

## BARBETTA
321 West 46th Street, 1931

Neon it's not, but Barbetta's elegant opalescent letter shadow box sign merits inclusion here as a kindred spirit, probably the last of its kind in New York. "Signs with raised opal glass letters are entirely obsolete in most places," explained one sign company in a brochure published in the early 1930s, "yet there are locations where the brilliant colors of neon are not desirable." Barbetta, it seems, was one such location. Opened in 1906 by Sebastiano Maioglio, today Barbetta advertises itself as "the oldest restaurant in New York that is still owned by its founding family." The sign dates to 1931. Its stylized silhouette and art deco edge molding are fine period details.

## BLOCK DRUGS
101 Second Avenue, 1945

The neon fascia sign of Block Drugs has presided over the intersection of Second Avenue and East Sixth Street since 1945, though the store dates to 1885. With its striking geometric sans-serif lettering outlined in neon tubes, this display speaks elegantly for the days before Helvetica.

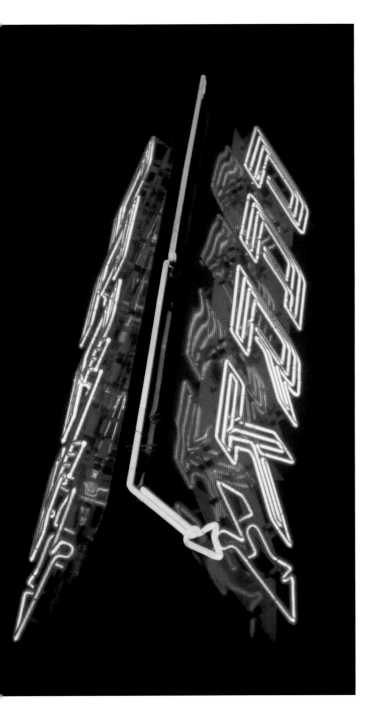

## BREVOORT GARAGE

21 East 12th Street, c. 1946*,
Serota Sign Corp.

Edsels and DeSotos once heeded
the clarion call of this fine garage
display at University Place and East
12th Street in Manhattan.

## BRIGHT FOOD SHOP

218 Eighth Avenue, 1948

An extravaganza of postwar
storefront neon marked the
northeasterly corner of Eighth
Avenue and West 21st Street for
some six decades until a rent hike
forced its owners to relinquish the
space in 2007. The sign survives,
under a tarp on an upstate farm.

## THE BROOKS ATKINSON THEATRE (FORMERLY THE MANSFIELD THEATRE)

256 West 37th Street, c. 1960*

Most of the old-timey exposed bulb
signs in New York's theater district
are imposters, having replaced
neon signs that predated them. The
Brooks Atkinson is one of a few
Broadway theaters that have kept
their neon signs in place. Built in
1926 as the Mansfield Theatre, it
was renamed in 1960 for outgoing
*New York Times* theater critic
Brooks Atkinson (1894-1984).

## C.O. BIGELOW CHEMISTS

414 Avenue of the Americas,
c. 1938*

The Bigelow sign hangs over the
entrance to Bigelow Chemists
from the façade of the Bigelow
Building. The business bills itself
as the second-oldest continuously-
operating pharmacy in the United
States, opened in 1838; the present
building, completed in 1902, is an
unusually elegant interpretation
of the prevailing neoclassical
vocabulary of its day. There is
nothing neoclassical about the
streamlined neon sign, installed
three decades later, but the two
seem happily in agreement today.

## CAMPANILE RESTAURANT (FORMERLY THE WEATHERVANE INN)

30 East 29th Street,
c. 1961*, Globe Neon Sign Co.

Faux-Colonial silhouette and blackletter type design recall the Weathervane Inn, which previously occupied this space tucked away on East 29th Street off Park Avenue.

## CAMBRIDGE WINE & LIQUOR

598 Eighth Avenue, 1952,
union sign shop no. 7

With its abstract silhouette and casual lettering, the vertical display of the Cambridge Wine and Liquor store is one of the more expressive surviving examples of 1950s liquor store signage in Manhattan today. It graces a still-gritty stretch of Eighth Avenue below the Port Authority Bus Terminal.

## CAPITOL FISHING TACKLE CO.

132 West 36th Street, 1941,
City Wide Neon Signs?

This venerable sign hints at the long and colorful past of the shop it advertises. Begun in Cologne, Germany, by Otto Neeff, the business and its founder relocated to New York in 1897. The sign appeared in 1941. Since then it has survived no fewer than three relocations of the specialty shop, first from its former location at East 34th Street and Third Avenue to a storefront at 219 Seventh Avenue in the early 1940s, then to the Chelsea Hotel where it operated from 1964 to 2006, and finally to its current home on West 36th Street. The store's owner, Richard Collins, hired Paul Signs of Brooklyn to carefully restore the sign during its most recent move.

## CARNEGIE DELICATESSEN

854 Seventh Avenue, c. 1960*,
Globe Neon Sign Co.

Opened in 1937, the Carnegie Deli takes its name from Carnegie Hall, a few blocks uptown. The sign, installed around 1960, is an unusual hybrid between back-lit acrylic panels and conventional sheet metal channel letters with exposed neon tubing, marking the transition away from neon during the period of its fabrication. Globe Neon installed a similar sign for the M&G Diner on West 125th Street (see page 88).

## CASA OLIVEIRA WINES AND LIQUORS

98 Seventh Avenue South,
1934 (swing), c. 1953 (fascia)

This neon swing sign predates the store's flashing fascia display by some two decades, but the pair make a pleasing ensemble today. The swing sign appeared with the opening of a liquor store here shortly after the repeal of Prohibition; the fascia sign was installed when the business changed hands around two decades later. LIQUORS and FINE WINES flash on and off in alternating sequence.

## CHARLES STREET GARAGE INC.

97 Charles Street, c. 1962*

Neon signs have long fascinated writers, painters, filmmakers, and photographers because of the delicate play of light and shadow that the signs cast across the facades from which they hang. The Charles Street Garage offers a particularly evocative example of this phenomenon in Greenwich Village.

## CHELSEA HOTEL

222 West 23rd Street, 1949

Neon and Queen Anne details set each other off nicely here. Built in 1883–1885 as one of the city's first apartment buildings, the Chelsea became a residential hotel in 1905. Later it hosted an array of noted artists and literati, from Bob Dylan to Dylan Thomas to Thomas Wolfe (though not in that order). Neon signs bedecked the lower reaches of the building's craggy facade by the 1940s, advertising an array of shops and restaurants that occupied the hotel's ground-level storefronts. Most of these have since departed, but the vertical sign advertising the hotel itself survives, its neon tubes as much interwoven with the fabric of the city's identity as any landmark of brick and mortar.

## CHRISTOPHER STREET WINE AND SPIRITS

45 Christopher Street

Streamlined lettering and border details suggest that this neon skeleton sign has been in place for a long time. Neon skeleton signs have changed little in the nearly nine decades that they have been common fixtures of downtown storefronts. Displayed from within the shelter of a climate-controlled environment, they can last many years with little or no maintenance.

## CINEMA VILLAGE

22 East 12th Street, c. 1964

A handsome juxtaposition of sleek 1960s script and block letters graces the marquee of the Cinema Village, opened as an art theater in 1964. It is one of the last traditional silhouette-letter marquees in town, the others having nearly all been replaced by LED displays.

## CLOVER
## DELICATESSEN

621 Second Avenue, 1956,
Globe Neon Sign Co.

Frank Cuttita opened the Clover
Delicatessen shortly after World
War II. Originally located at 572
Second Avenue, the establishment
took its name from the popular
song "I'm Looking over a Four
Leaf Clover," a rendition of which
by Art Mooney reached number
one on the charts in early 1948.
Twice displaced by urban renewal
projects, the shop finally settled at
the southwest corner of Second
Avenue and East 34th Street around
1955. It has been managed by the
Cuttita family for four generations.

## THE COFFEE SHOP
## (FORMERLY CHASE
## COFFEE SHOP)

29 Union Square West, c. 1960*

This landmark sign once advertised
the Chase Coffee Shop, which
opened here c. 1960.

# COLLINS BAR

735 Eighth Avenue, c. 1930

The Collins Bar disappeared quietly in the summer of 2007, taking with it one of New York's oldest neon signs, probably fabricated c. 1930.

The sign marked the spot of an unpretentious watering hole that had occupied the same space for generations.

## COLUMBUS HARDWARE

852 Ninth Avenue, 1955

Ninth Avenue is known as Columbus Avenue only above West 59th Street, but Columbus Hardware braces uptown-bound pedestrians for the impending change three blocks in advance. The sign's rose-colored fluorescent tubes contrast vibrantly with its canary yellow porcelain-enamel sheet metal.

## DUBLIN HOUSE BAR

225 West 79th Street, 1933,
E. G. Clarke Inc.

The Dublin House and its sign have been in place since 1933. The sign is the work of E. G. Clarke Inc., which later went on to collaborate with Douglas Leigh on some of the lesser-known Times Square spectaculars. A striking creation, the Dublin House's neon harp earned itself a small feature in *Signs of the Times* magazine at the time of its installation.

## CORK AND BOTTLE LIQUOR STORE

1158 First Avenue, c. 1940*
(vertical), 1970; Laster Neon
Engineering Co. (raceway)

Two generations of neon signs hang over this Upper East Side storefront. Streamlined geometry and fine stainless-steel details identify the vertical display as the older of the two.

## EAST 43RD
## STREET GARAGE
**217 East 43rd Street, c. 1959***

Like many Manhattan parking
garages, this one began life as a
livery stable, built in 1907. The neon
sign appeared around 1959. Its
bold, italic lettering speaks for the
forward look of the period.

## EAR
## INN
**326 Spring Street, c. 1945**

This classic swing sign hangs
from the front of a Federal
style townhouse built in 1817.
Known for many years only as
"The Green Door," the ground
floor bar served longshoremen
from the nearby North River
piers. The establishment took
its present name in 1977 under
new management, purportedly
so the owners could avoid
subjecting a new sign to review
by the Landmarks Preservation
Commission.

# EL QUIJOTE RESTAURANT

226 West 23rd Street,
c. 1947*

Open since 1930, El Quijote bills itself as New York's oldest Spanish restaurant. It has long served as the Chelsea Hotel's on-premises restaurant and bar. The sign exhibits inventive script lettering with distinctive stainless-steel details to either side.

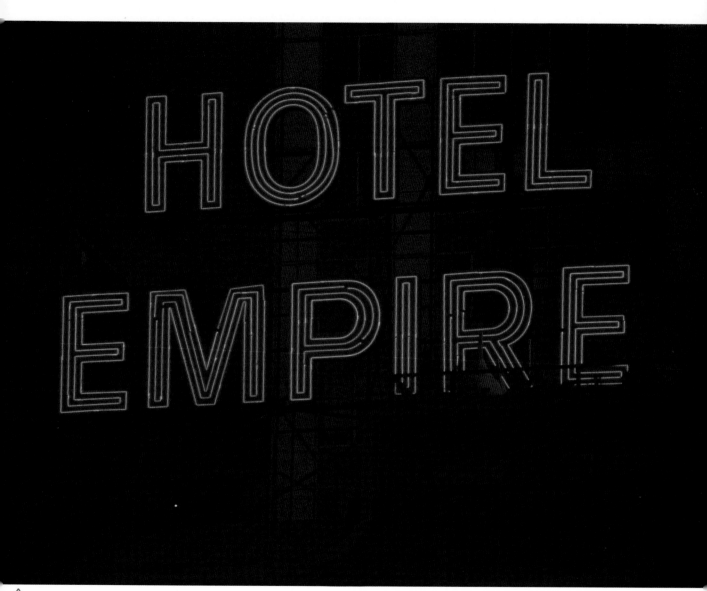

## EMPIRE HOTEL

**44 West 63rd Street, c. 1930
(reconstructed, c. 1966\*)**

The existing roof signs atop the Empire Hotel echo similar signs that appeared atop the building a few years after its construction in 1923. Whereas such signs were once standard equipment for many urban hotels, today these are among the very last to grace the New York skyline. Happily, the building's owners retained and restored the signs as part of a major overhaul of the Empire in 2007–2008.

### ESSEX HOUSE

160 Central Park South, c. 1932

The Essex House and its sign reared
their heads above the treetops of
Central Park in the early 1930s. The
sign's giant channel letters were
originally illuminated from within,
but they are now lit by floodlights
projecting up from the building's
roof. A legend within New York's
sign industry holds that electricians
wired its letters so that transformer
outages might give strollers in the
park something to talk about.

### FAMOUS OYSTER BAR

842 Seventh Avenue, c. 1960

The bright signs of this corner
restaurant near Carnegie Hall have
been a neighborhood landmark for
more than half a century. The swing
sign has apparently been re-lettered
from a previous incarnation.

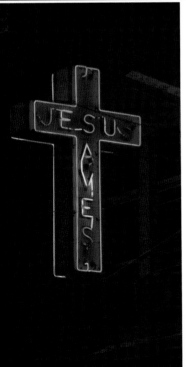

### THE FATHER'S HEART MINISTRIES

545 East 11th Street,
c. 1965

Founded in 1919, this claims the distinction of being the "first Slavic Pentecostal Church in America." The church boasts one of a small handful of neon crucifixes that continue to light the way in the twenty-first century. Once, these signs were common: New York Edison had counted more than one hundred illuminated signs for churches in Manhattan below 135th Street in 1927. New York's largest illuminated crucifix may have been one that once stood atop the Seaman's Church Institute in lower Manhattan, which was switched on by President Calvin Coolidge in a ceremony on Good Friday, 1927.

### FANELLI CAFÉ

94 Prince Street, c. 1955,
West Side Neon Sign Corp.

This bar and grill at the corner of Prince and Mercer streets has lived through dramatic changes in the character of its surrounding neighborhood. It had already been here for decades when Michael Fanelli took it over and gave it its present name in 1922. The neon sign over its door is one of the very few concessions to progress that Mr. Fanelli allowed here in the six decades he ran the business.

## FEDORA RESTAURANT

**239 West 4th Street, c. 1947**

This sign originally advertised a restaurant called Bill and Jerry's, which operated in the basement of this historic Greenwich Village rowhouse for a few years after World War II. In 1952 the business reopened as Fedora, named for Fedora Dorato, who managed the restaurant with her husband. The sign was re-lettered accordingly. Mrs. Dorato continued to run the restaurant after her husband's death, finally retiring in 2010 after some fifty-eight years. The business has since reopened under the same name, but with new management, updated decor, a vastly reconfigured menu, and a facsimile of the restaurant's old sign.

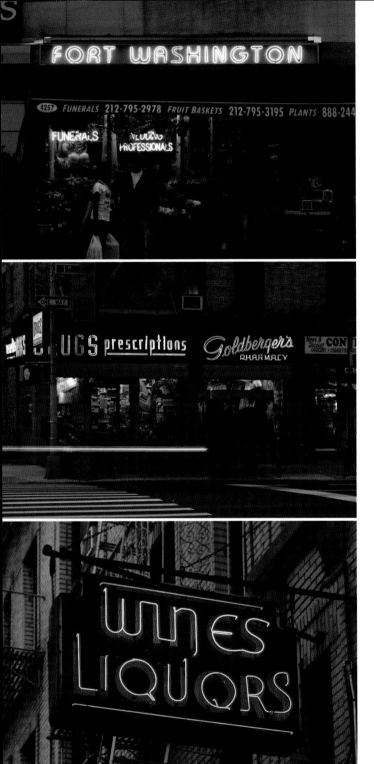

## FORT WASHINGTON FLORIST

4257 Broadway, c. 1950

Handsome lettering outlined in white neon tubes enlivens this otherwise ordinary block in the Fort Washington section of Manhattan.

## GOLDBERGER'S PHARMACY

1200 First Avenue, c. 1960

Goldberger's Pharmacy traces its origins to 1898. Its neon fascia sign stands out as something of an antique in the twenty-first century, but it must have struck some as a bold new look for an establishment that had already been in business more than fifty years before the sign appeared.

## GOLDEN RULE WINE AND LIQUOR

457 Hudson Street, 1934,
Neon Sign & Service Co.

The especially handsome swing sign over this storefront may have been a catalog item: historic photographs show signs of the same streamlined design in various locations throughout the city. The others are gone now, but this one remains in service nearly eight decades after its installation.

## GREYSTONE HOTEL
### 212 West 91st Street, c. 1964*

As New York's so-called SRO ("single room occupancy") hotels went, the Greystone had a fairly good reputation, with university students and senior citizens making up the better part of its clientele. SROs could once be found in many parts of the city, but they were especially concentrated on Manhattan's Upper West Side. Typically, these were once-stately hotels that incrementally transformed into cheap apartment buildings as business declined with the opening of newer hotels and a general downturn in New York's tourist trade. Old neon signs left over from better days made for one of their quintessential hallmarks. Amid surging real estate prices in the 1990s, the SROs of the Upper West Side disappeared en masse and were gut-renovated and reborn as high-end hotels or luxury condominiums. The Greystone eventually made this transition in 2008, but it kept its sign in place.

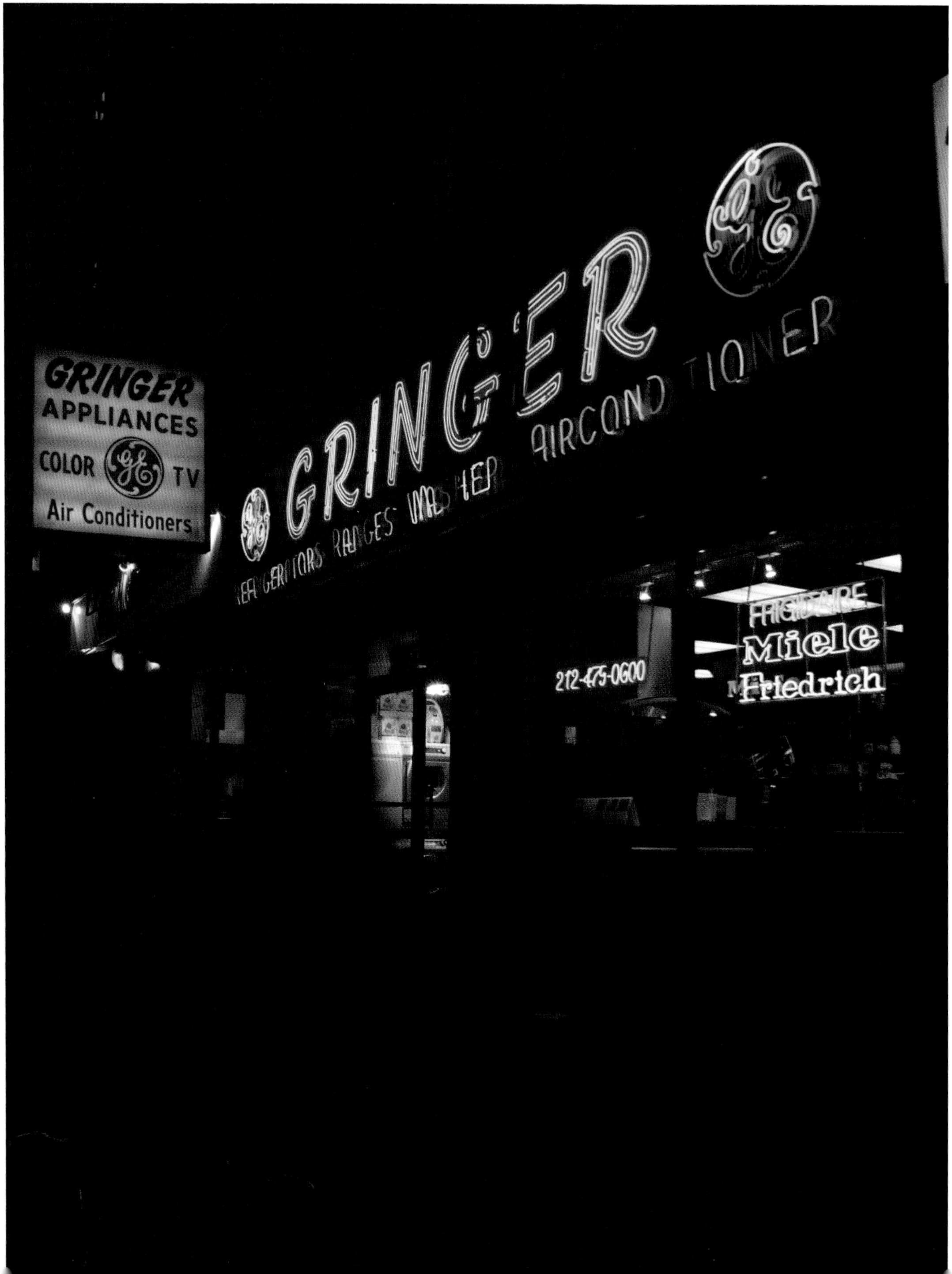
GRINGER
APPLIANCES
COLOR TV
Air Conditioners
GRINGER
AIRCONDITIONER
212-475-0600
Miele
Friedrich

## GRINGER APPLIANCES

27 First Avenue, 1953,
Salzman Sign Co.

This business originally opened in
1918, and its neon sign has been a
beacon of home appliance retailing
for nearly sixty years. The sign was
carefully restored by Let There Be
Neon in 2007.

## S&G GROSS CO.

486 Eighth Avenue, c. 1959,
Grauer Sign Co.

Everything about the neon sign and
porcelain-enamel facade cladding
this three-story building suggests a
1930s alteration, but records at the
Department of Buildings indicate a
surprisingly late installation date of
1959. Like neon signs, pawnbrokers
have long been the subject of
fanciful if generally unflattering
characterizations conjured up by
and for the American mainstream.
This seems not to have hampered
business at S&G Gross, which
celebrated its centennial in 2001.

## HOUSE OF WINE AND LIQUOR
**250 East 34th Street, 1959**

A slender luminous arrow points the way to this store near the corner of Second Avenue and East 34th Street.

## KATZ'S DELICATESSEN
**205 East Houston Street, 1935, AAA Neon Sign Company**

In business since 1888, Katz's commodious deli-cafeteria on Manhattan's Lower East Side ranks as one of New York's most venerable commercial institutions. The neon sign is one of many once-common accoutrements here that now stand out for their rarity; other bygone items include wooden telephone booths, streamlined chrome water fountains, and a take-a-ticket ordering system.

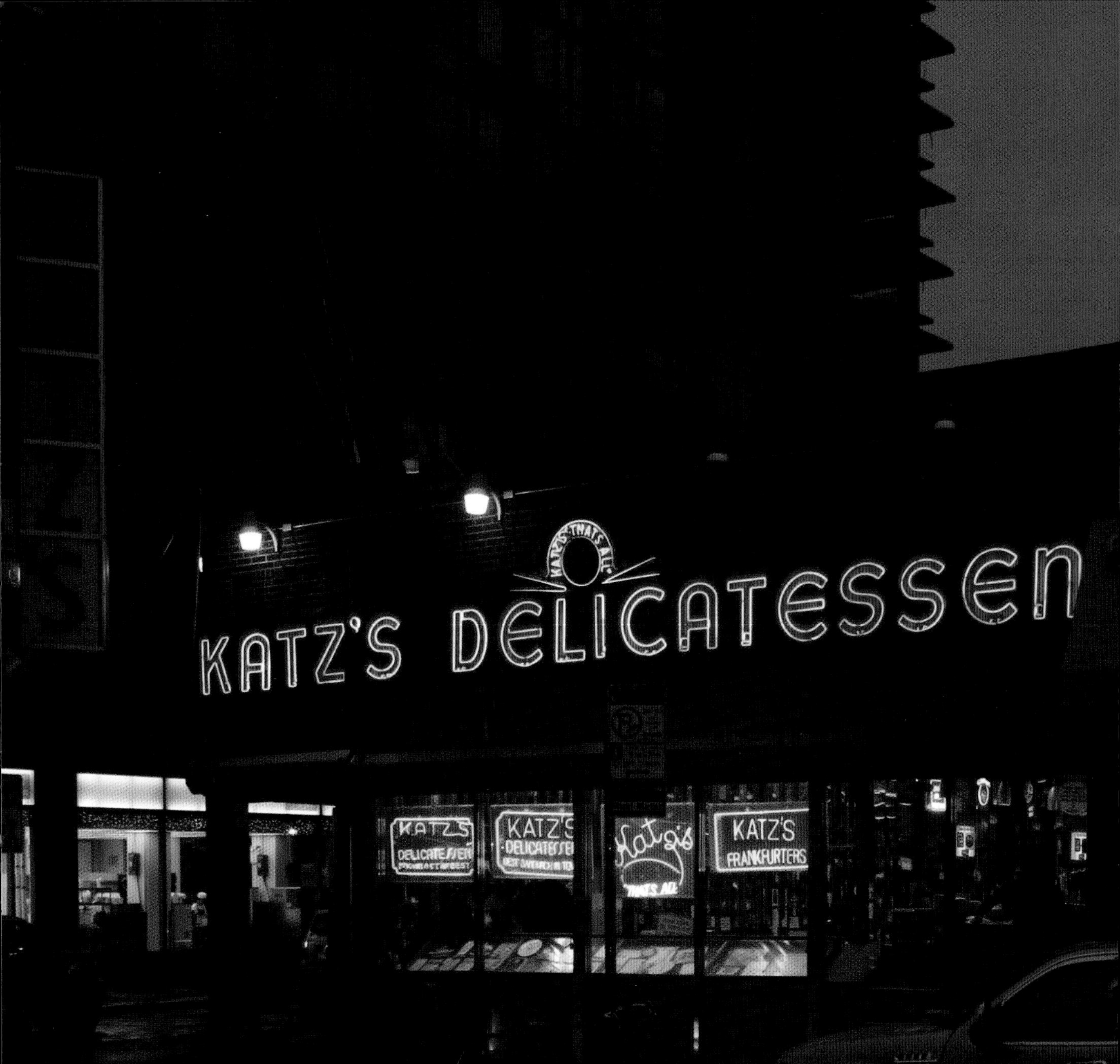
KATZ'S DELICATESSEN
KATZ'S
KATZ'S
KATZ'S
FRANKFURTERS

## KELLER
## HOTEL

150 Barrow Street, 1933,
Beacon Neon Corp.

Opened in 1898, the Keller belonged
to a battery of waterfront hostelries
that stood opposite the headhouses
of the North River steamship
piers, catering to passengers and
merchant seamen coming and going
from what was once the world's
busiest port. With the dramatic
decline in harbor traffic after World
War II, waterfront hotels like the
Keller fell on hard times: many
closed or, like this one, became
so-called SROs that provided
meager accommodation for tenants
of very limited means. Heightened
demand for waterfront real estate
has since displaced most of these
establishments and their residents.
Given Landmark status in 2007, the
Keller has sat empty for a number of
years and awaits redevelopment.

## J. LEON LASCOFF
## AND SON

1209 Lexington Avenue,
1931

The poet Charles Greene Shaw
wrote of his admiration for an old
wooden mortar and pestle sign he
found advertising this Upper East
Side chemist's in 1938, but he
did not remark on the neon sign
that had gone up beside it seven
years earlier. Today the mortar and
pestle is gone, but Lascoff's neon
sign (sans tubes) remains in place,
now as much a curiosity as its
predecessor.

## LA PARISIENNE
## COFFEE HOUSE

910 Seventh Avenue,
c. 1968*

La Parisienne offers a haven of
down-to-earth hospitality in a part
of midtown Manhattan where ultra-
high rents leave almost no room for
even remotely ephemeral parts of
the urban landscape. Open since
1950, La Parisienne's sign appeared
roughly two decades later.

## LENOX LOUNGE

288 Lenox Avenue,
c. 1955

Originally opened as the Lenox
Bar-B-Q in 1939, this later
became known as Lenox Lounge,
an intimate venue for live
performances by John Coltrane,
Miles Davis, Billie Holiday, and
others in the 1950s. The moderne
porcelain-enamel and stainless-
steel facade is possibly the finest
surviving example of 1930s
storefront architecture in New York
today. The neon fascia sign above
postdates the storefront but it is no
less appealing.

## LIVE BAIT BAR AND RESTAURANT

14 East 23rd Street, c. 1941* (vertical), c. 1955 (raceway)

Just steps away from the very spot where the world's first commercial electric sign beckoned the likes of Theodore Dreiser in the early 1890s, this display is about all that remains to echo the days when sedate Madison Square pulsed with the rhythm of the city's theater and entertainment district. Records at the Department of Buildings indicate that the vertical sign appeared in 1941 to advertise an establishment known as the Metro Tavern. The existing raceway sign covers an earlier neon fascia sign.

## MANGANARO FOODS AND RESTAURANT

488 Ninth Avenue, c. 1955

This Italian grosseria traced its roots to 1893, when the Petrucci family set up shop here. Ownership passed to the Manganaro family in the 1920s. The business boasted one of the last neon signs in New York to flash rhythmically on and off. This store closed in 2012, ending a 119-year run.

## MINETTA TAVERN

113 Macdougal Street, c. 1950

Opened in 1937, the tavern received a thorough makeover in 2008 after being acquired by the restaurateur Keith McNally, whose affinity for old neon can be traced back to the opening of his first restaurant—the Odeon—in 1980. The neon tubes outlining the word RESTAURANT, formerly green, now glow in a vivid shade of red.

## M&G DINER

383 West 125th Street, c. 1966*, Globe Neon Sign Co.

The M&G Diner billed its cuisine as "old fashion' BUT Good!" right up until the day it closed in the summer of 2008. By that time the slogan applied as much to its signs as to the soul food it advertised.

## METROPOLITAN LIFE INSURANCE COMPANY

200 Park Avenue, 1992–1993,
Universal Unlimited

This display is the successor to the landmark Pan Am sign that had beamed out from atop the eponymous tower for nearly thirty years. For obstructing the vista up and down Park Avenue, critics had maligned both tower and sign at the time of their completion in 1963. In the decades since then, the building has been slow to endear itself to anyone. But the Pan Am sign became the subject of much lament when it was taken down after the airline's bankruptcy in 1992. "Couldn't they just leave the sign up and take the building down?" remarked Robert A. M. Stern at the time. Fortunately, the MetLife sign has filled this prominent niche, albeit without the stylish serifs of its predecessor.

## MANLEY'S WINE AND SPIRITS

35 Eighth Avenue,
c. 1934*

Manley's opened its doors shortly after the repeal of Prohibition in the early 1930s. The sign was rebuilt in recent years but retains its original appearance.

## MILFORD PLAZA HOTEL (FORMERLY THE HOTEL MANHATTAN)

700 Eighth Avenue, 1958,
Artkraft Strauss Sign Corp.

The giant M atop the Milford Plaza survived from the hotel's previous incarnation as the Hotel Manhattan. The display was floodlit in recent years, but in its original glory it stood bedecked in some 6,500 feet of neon tubes that changed color from white and gold to blue. The building originally opened in 1928 as the Hotel Lincoln. Artkraft Strauss installed the big "M" when the hostelry was first re-branded in 1958, just two years after the firm created the great Pepsi-Cola waterfall spectacular in Times Square, one block to the east. The big M vanished in 2011 during a major renovation of the hotel beneath.

## MISHKIN'S DRUG STORE

1714 Amsterdam Avenue, 1950,
Serota Sign Corp.

Mishkin's dates its origins to 1890. The neon sign has anchored this corner for about half that time.

### MITCHELL'S WINE AND LIQUOR STORE

200 West 86th Street, 1946 (fascia), Midtown Neon Sign Corp. (vertical, 1949)

Patrons of this Upper West Side liquor store recognize its sign by a distinctive diacritical dot in blue neon that is nested between the words WINES and LIQUORS. Channel letters in appealing midcentury lettering reside on a backing of black Carrara-pigmented structural glass.

### MONTE'S TRATTORIA

97 Macdougal Street, c. 1955

Monte's takes its name from the Monteverde family, which opened this staple of Greenwich Village red-sauce fare in 1918. The restaurant's current proprietor, Pietro Mosconi, came to New York from Italy aboard the SS *Michelangelo* in 1966, and took over the restaurant from the descendants of the original owners in the early 1980s.

### NEIL'S COFFEE SHOP

961 Lexington Avenue, c. 1966*

A simple but distinctive neon swing sign brightens the southeast corner of Lexington Avenue and East 70th Street where this shop has served locals and visitors for more than two generations.

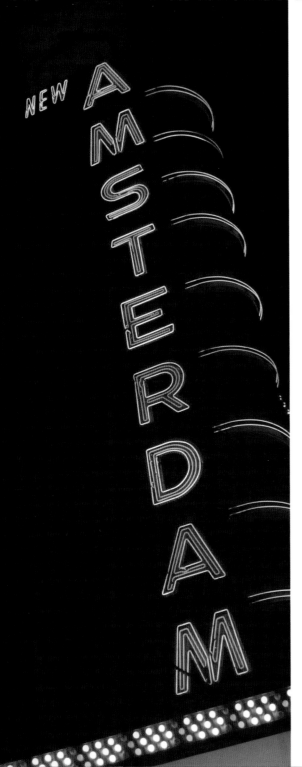

# NEW AMSTERDAM THEATRE

214 West 42nd Street,
1937 (alterations, 1955),
Artkraft Strauss Sign Corp.

Times Square was still known as
Longacre Square when the New
Amsterdam Theatre opened in
1903. With seats for more than
1,700, it was the largest theater
in the city at the time of its
completion. After closing briefly
during the Great Depression, it
reopened in 1937 as a movie house.
The vertical sign over its entrance
dates from this time. Alterations
in 1955 gave the sign its stainless-
steel-framed clock (at top) and sans-
serif lettering. In 1997 the New
Amsterdam reopened again, leased
to the Disney Corporation, which
has brought live performances back
to its stage. Though some favored
removing the 1930s marquee to
restore the theater's facade to its
original appearance, cooler heads
prevailed and the historic signs
were restored along with the rest of
the theater.

⇧

## NEW YORK POLICE DEPARTMENT (TIMES SQUARE KIOSK)

Times Square, c. 1980

Mosaic maps highlighting New York landmarks denote this building's origins as the Times Square Information Center, opened in 1957. Its installation displaced one of the most heavily used entrances to the Times Square subway station, along with one of the subway's original cast-iron entrance pavilions. The building was given over to the NYPD around 1980, as the city prepared to launch a comprehensive cleanup of Times Square. With LEDs now illuminating nearly all of Times Square's great spectaculars, this animated raceway sign is now one of the square's last vestiges of traditional exposed-tube neon. This sign made way for a facsimile by the Lettera Sign Co., installed in time for New Year's Eve 2011

# NORTH VILLAGE WINE AND LIQUOR

254 West 14th Street, c. 1950

Stainless-steel details embellish this impressive vertical sign, which has beckoned generations of thirsty bargain hunters to the corner of West 14th Street and Eighth Avenue.

## THE OLD HOMESTEAD STEAK HOUSE

56 Ninth Avenue, c. 1945

"Established 1868" says this neon sign, attesting to the longevity of the Old Homestead Steakhouse in the meatpacking district. The restaurant has now outlived nearly all of the businesses that gave this area its name.

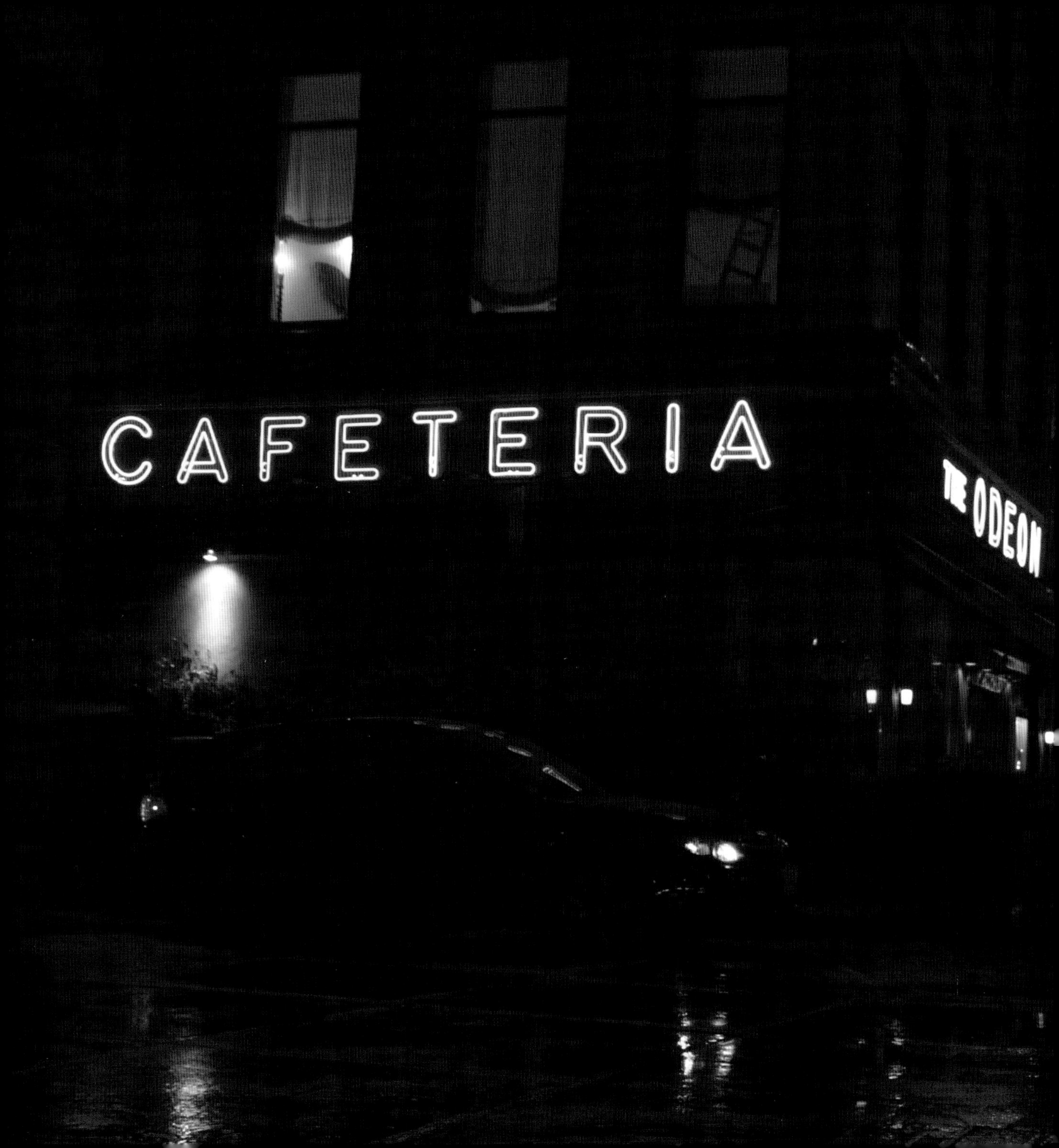
CAFETERIA
THE ODEON

## THE ODEON RESTAURANT

145 West Broadway, 1933,
Astor Neon Sign Co.

In a past life this sophisticated
French bistro existed as the
Towers Cafeteria, which opened
in 1933. A story published in *Signs
of the Times* that year described
this installation as the product of
"considerable heated competition
among sign manufacturers for
the business, not competition on
the subject of price, as is usually
the case, but competition on the
basis of the display's design and
construction." The restaurateur
Keith McNally preserved the
old cafeteria's porcelain-enamel
storefront in the eatery's
metamorphosis in 1980. McNally
modified one of the sign's faces to
reflect the restaurant's new name,
but he left the other unchanged.
Still among New York's most
distinctive on-premise displays,
this is also one of the city's oldest
surviving neon signs.

⇑

## ORTHODOX CATHEDRAL OF THE HOLY VIRGIN PROTECTION

59 East 2nd Street, c. 1945

A patriarchal cross in white
fluorescent neon identifies the
Orthodox Cathedral of the Holy
Virgin Protection on East 2nd
Street. Like the Father's Heart
church on East 11th Street (see
page 76), this institution connotes
the area's once dense population
of Eastern European immigrants.
Formerly known as the Church of
St. Nicholas, the parish previously
had its headquarters on East 97th
Street, before moving to its present
home in 1942. The building itself
began life as the Olivet Memorial
Church, completed in 1892 to plans
by the noted architect J. Cleaveland
Cady, whose works also included
the original Metropolitan Opera
House (1883, demolished 1967)
and the imposing south elevation
of the American Museum of Natural
History (1887–1901).

## OLD TOWN BAR

45 East 18th Street,
1937

A bar and grill of one sort or another had already operated here for more than forty years when the Old Town hung this neon sign over its door in 1937. Originally a German saloon called Veimeister's, the business operated inconspicuously as "Craig's Restaurant" during Prohibition before taking its current name in 1933. The neon sign remains one of a very few gestures this establishment has made to the changing world outside. In 2008 the sign received a thorough refurbishment by Let There Be Neon.

## P&G BAR

279 Amsterdam Avenue, 1947,
union sign shop no. 17

By the time the P&G closed its doors in January 2009, the bar was known throughout the city for its elaborate neon fascia sign, whose good looks had earned it cameos in motion pictures, various television series, and at least one music video. Though not extraordinary by the standards of its day, the sign was widely considered one of New York's finest specimens of historic on-premise advertising by the time of its demise. The establishment took its name from Pete and George Chahalis, whose father, Tom, had opened the bar in 1942.

## PAPAYA KING

179 East 86th Street, 1964,
LaSalle Sign Corp.

The Papaya King's fascia signs are notable for their inventive lettering, which is likely the work of Samuel Langsner, who designed this display in 1964. The business began as Hawaiian Tropical Drinks, a juice bar opened in 1931. Within a few years it became known for specializing in the unlikely combination of papaya juice and hot dogs. The idea caught on, eventually spawning numerous spin-offs and knock-offs, and the "papaya dog" has become something of a New York specialty today.

# PARKSIDE LOUNGE

317 East Houston Street,
1955

Known these days as a venue
for miscellaneous live bands and
standup comics, the Parkside
Lounge occupies a humble
structure at the corner of East
Houston and Attorney streets on
the Lower East Side. The building's
two-piece neon sign is its most
distinctive feature. Like many
signs of its period, this one gives
prominent billing to the building's
street address.

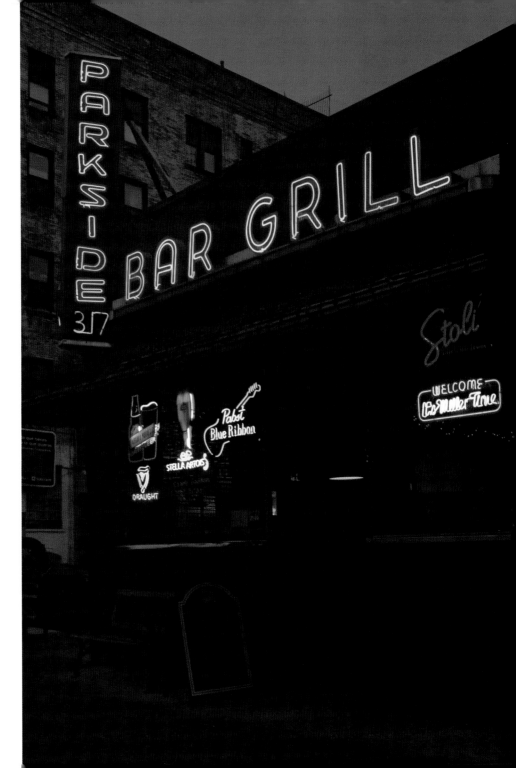

## PATSY'S ITALIAN RESTAURANT

236 West 56th Street, 1954,
Serota Sign Corp.?

Manhattan boasts not one but
two venerable Italian restaurants
called Patsy's. The midtown Patsy's
offers this ensemble of elegant
neon signs on West 56th Street.
Originally opened in 1944, the
restaurant moved to its current
location ten years later.

## PEARL STREET DINER

212 Pearl Street, 1958,
union sign shop no. 2

Standing humbly in the shadows
of lower Manhattan's tall towers,
the little Pearl Street Diner has
occupied this corner since 1958.
The building has been substantially
altered since it first opened, but its
neon sign remains from the diner's
original configuration.

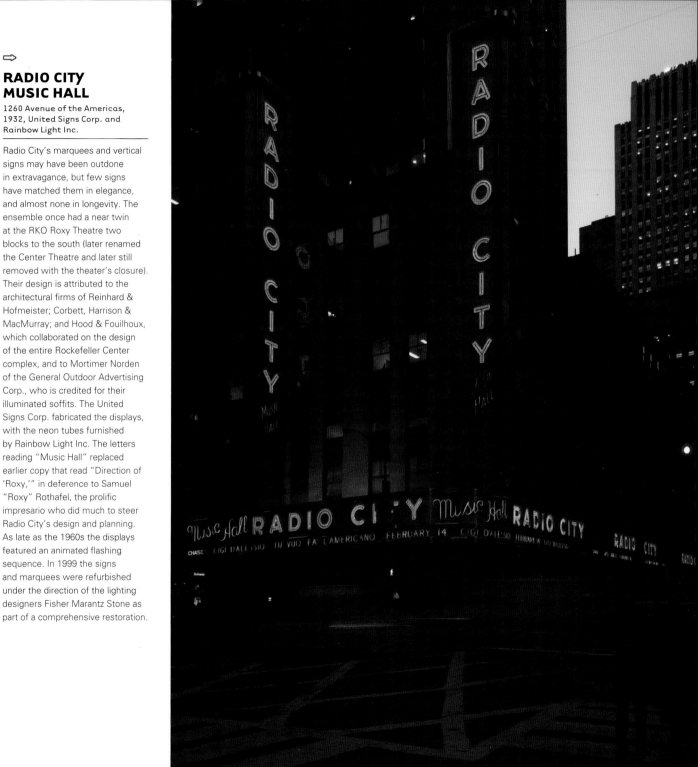

## RADIO CITY MUSIC HALL

1260 Avenue of the Americas,
1932, United Signs Corp. and
Rainbow Light Inc.

Radio City's marquees and vertical signs may have been outdone in extravagance, but few signs have matched them in elegance, and almost none in longevity. The ensemble once had a near twin at the RKO Roxy Theatre two blocks to the south (later renamed the Center Theatre and later still removed with the theater's closure). Their design is attributed to the architectural firms of Reinhard & Hofmeister; Corbett, Harrison & MacMurray; and Hood & Fouilhoux, which collaborated on the design of the entire Rockefeller Center complex, and to Mortimer Norden of the General Outdoor Advertising Corp., who is credited for their illuminated soffits. The United Signs Corp. fabricated the displays, with the neon tubes furnished by Rainbow Light Inc. The letters reading "Music Hall" replaced earlier copy that read "Direction of 'Roxy,'" in deference to Samuel "Roxy" Rothafel, the prolific impresario who did much to steer Radio City's design and planning. As late as the 1960s the displays featured an animated flashing sequence. In 1999 the signs and marquees were refurbished under the direction of the lighting designers Fisher Marantz Stone as part of a comprehensive restoration.

(clockwise from top left):

## RIVERSIDE LIQUOR CO.
2746 Broadway, 1955

## McKEY LIQUORS INC.
308 86th Street, Brooklyn, c. 1962
(facsimile, c. 2000 by Paul Signs)

## GOLDEN RULE WINE AND LIQUOR
457 Hudson Street, c. 1960*
(fascia)

## JL WINE AND LIQUORS (FORMERLY GOLDRICH WINES)
60 East 34th Street, 1950

## KESSLER LIQUORS
23 East 28th Street, 1959

## CAMBRIDGE WINE AND LIQUOR
598 Eighth Avenue, 1952

Liquor stores did not exist (at least not legally) when neon first appeared in the United States during Prohibition. After repeal, neon was widely adopted. Like neon signs for parking garages, those installed for liquor stores have had enjoyed a much higher-than-average life expectancy as these examples (including the interloper from Brooklyn) attest. It helps that many feature generic copy (LIQUORS, WINES & LIQUORS, LIQUOR STORE) that remains current should the business change its name or ownership.

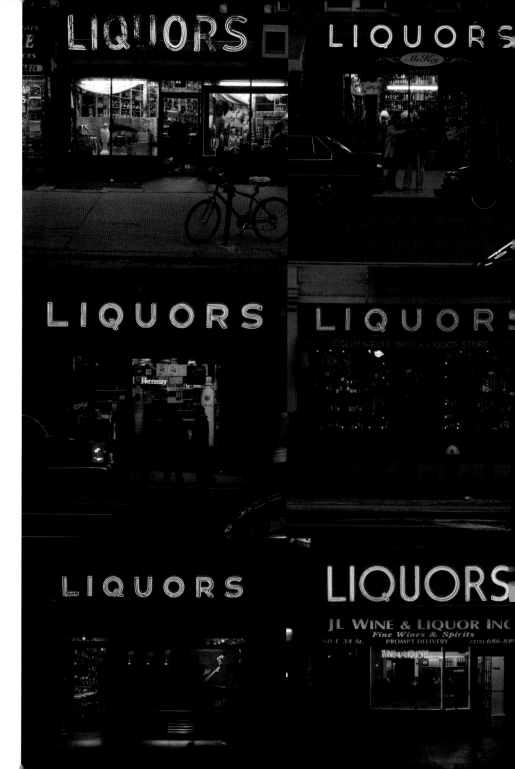

## THE RAINBOW ROOM

30 Rockefeller Plaza,
c. 1935

Situated sixty-five floors above
the street, the Rainbow Room is
known to most passersby only
by its distinctive marquee, which
also heralds the entrance to NBC
studios, housed in the same
building. The letters OBSERVATION
DECK are a recent addition, having
appeared when the building's roof
terrace reopened in 2005.

## REYNOLDS CAFÉ

710 West 180th Street, c. 1959*
(altered c. 1964)

Reynolds Café has occupied the
corner of Broadway and West
180th Street in the Washington
Heights section of Manhattan
since 1964. Previously it was
known as Bill's Café, which
likely accounts for the ghosts of
abandoned electrode housings on
the sign's south-facing exposure.

⇐

# HOTEL ROGER SMITH

501 Lexington Avenue, c. 1950

Years after long-distance passenger trains ceased using Grand Central Terminal, Lexington Avenue above 42nd Street is still lined with an impressive row of grand old hotels that have remained viable despite the loss of business that was once provided by the railroad. These include the Waldorf-Astoria at East 49th Street; the architect Morris Lapidus's Summit Hotel at East 51st Street; and the Roger Smith, at East 47th Street. Built in 1925, the Roger Smith can be spotted by its tall, slender neon sign, nearly six stories high, which is still clearly visible from Grand Central.

## ROCCO RISTORANTE

181 Thompson Street, 1934

Rocco Stanzione opened the restaurant that bore his name in 1922; it remained under the management of his descendants until the owners called it quits in 2012, citing a steep rent hike. The hand-painted neon sign had hung over its door since 1934.

## ROSE WINE AND LIQUOR CORP.

449 Columbus Avenue, c. 1954*, Midtown Neon Sign Co.

Red neon tubes densely packed into stainless-steel channel letters set against a backing of deep blue porcelain enamel mark the spot of the Rose Wine and Liquor Corp., one block up Columbus Avenue from the Museum of Natural History.

## RUDY'S BAR AND GRILL

627 Ninth Avenue, 1937

This neon sign once cast its glow through the riveted steel tracery of the Ninth Avenue El. Its distinctive silhouette and bold white-on-black lettering make this sign an exemplary period piece. The sign was commissioned in 1937 for Helen Rudy, whose family's bar and grill opened at this location four years earlier. Mrs. Rudy's son, Jack, began tending bar here in 1943, at age sixteen, and continues to manage the business nearly seven decades later.

## RUSS AND DAUGHTERS

179 East Houston Street, 1951

Happy neon fish glow over the entrance to Russ and Daughters, an institution of Lower East Side Judaica that has operated under the management of four generations of the same family since it opened in 1914. Originally located on Orchard Street, the business has occupied this storefront on East Houston Street since 1920. Its specialties include smoked salmon and herring, caviar, and bagels and lox. The sign underwent a careful restoration by Let There Be Neon in 2008.

## SARDI'S

**234 West 44th Street, 1937**

Vincent Sardi Sr. founded this restaurant's predecessor in 1921. It assumed its present form in 1927, when new construction during the building boom of the roaring twenties displaced Mr. Sardi's restaurant from its original address down the street. The sign appeared ten years later, by which time Sardi's was well on its way to becoming a sort of sanctum sanctorum of the theater district. Its design is attributed to the architect Francis Gina, Vincent Sardi's brother-in-law, a prominent designer of storefronts.

## 79TH STREET WINE AND SPIRITS

230 West 79th Street, c. 1950,
Da Nite Neon Signs (vertical)

Vertical and horizontal neon signs brighten the sidewalk in front of 79th Street Wine and Spirits.

## SEWARD PARK LIQUORS INC.

393 Grand Street, 1960

Seward Park Liquors has been under the same ownership since 1973. The neon sign is older. The shop occupies a single-story commercial building constructed as part of Seward Park Houses, one of several complexes of high-rise apartment buildings planned in the 1950s under the auspices of various labor unions and other nonprofit organizations to provide affordable housing for middle-income families.

## SMITH'S BAR AND RESTAURANT

801 Eighth Avenue, 1954,
Da Nite Neon Signs

Situated just west of Times Square, Smith's Bar once shared this stretch of Eighth Avenue with a notorious lineup of down-and-out dives, adult movie theaters, and flophouses. In recent years the street has cleaned up measurably. The few adult "novelty" shops and peep shows that survive here seem almost quaint, regarded by both native New Yorkers and European tourists with a strange nostalgic affection. Through all of this, Smith's survives, though it, too, has experienced a bit of a facelift in recent years.

## SUBWAY INN

143 East 60th Street, 1950
(vertical), c. 1955, Serota Sign
Corp.? (fascia)

Here in the shadow of Bloomingdale's lies a place sheltered from the whims of fashion, a comfortable outpost for those ill at ease amid the pretensions of Manhattan's well-to-do Upper East Side. The bar takes its name from the underground junction of the IRT and BMT subways almost directly beneath the jukebox by the door. Originally opened around 1934, the bar's ownership passed to Charlie Akerman after World War II, who commissioned the existing signs a few years later. Mr. Akerman ran the bar for nearly sixty years until his death at ninety-seven. A partnership of longtime bartenders took up the management thereafter.

## SUPERIOR FLORIST LTD.

828 Avenue of the Americas, 1951,
Salzman Sign Co.

Manhattan once sorted itself out into
various "districts" where businesses
of certain typologies gathered more
or less spontaneously. Most of
these have scattered to the winds
since the city's economic recovery
in recent decades, but the flower
district is still alive and well in the
twenty-first century. Superior Florist
boasts perhaps the most memorable
of several fine old storefronts to
be found here. The sign dates to
1951; the business is older, founded
in 1930.

## TOM'S RESTAURANT

2880 Broadway, 1957

Originally installed for the Columbia Restaurant, this fascia sign became familiar throughout the world as the fictional "Monk's Restaurant," featured in most episodes of the television sitcom *Seinfeld*, which aired from 1989 to 1998. Earlier, the restaurant was the subject of Suzanne Vega's song "Tom's Diner," penned in 1981.

## 20TH CENTURY GARAGE

### 320 East 48th Street, c. 1960

The 20th Century Garage may have taken its name from the luxurious 20th Century Limited, which passengers could board just a few blocks away at Grand Central Terminal. The New York Central Railroad scratched the Century from its timetables in 1967, but one can still find parking at this garage more than forty years later.

## 3139 BROADWAY LIQUORS

3139 Broadway, c. 1955

Complementary hues of faded blue paint and rusted sheet metal lend a fine weather-beaten character to the faces of this vertical display, which has overlooked the elevated tracks of the IRT subway for more than fifty years.

## HOTEL TUDOR

304 East 42nd Street, c. 1940

The Hotel Tudor opened in 1932, rounding out the urban enclave of Tudor City. The building's most distinctive feature may be its neon roof sign, styled in the shape of a suggestive capital T, which beckoned would-be guests from Grand Central Terminal just a few blocks west on 42nd Street. The sign remained lit until the hotel's acquisition by the Hilton Hotel Corp. in 2010. Hilton rebranded the establishment the "Hilton Manhattan East" and extinguished the sign after some seventy years of brightening the midtown skyline, echoing lingering corporate misgivings toward neon that are as old as the sign itself. Fortunately, the building is protected as part of the Tudor City Historic District, meaning that any changes to the sign would be subject to the city's Landmarks Commission.

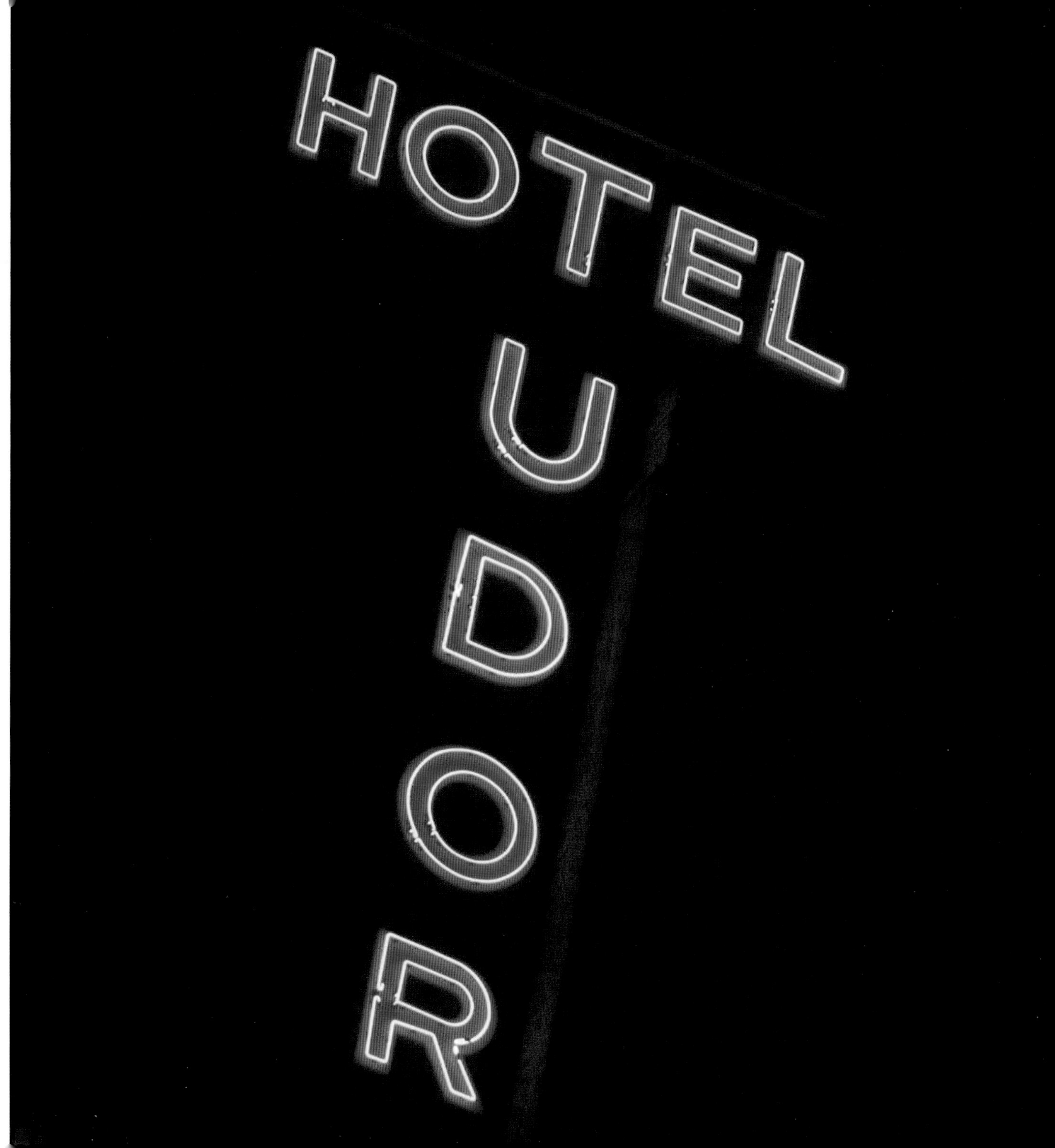
HOTEL
TUDOR

## TUDOR CITY

45 Tudor City Place, 1939,
Claude Neon Lights Inc.

Electric roof signs for apartment
buildings are somewhat common in
Los Angeles, but they never really
caught on in New York. Built in
1925–1928 by the developer Fred
F. French, Tudor City was perhaps
the most prominent of many
"apartment villages" to appear in
New York during the interwar years.
Shortly after its completion, French
installed large twin roof signs
atop two of the complex's three
towers, oriented to face west down
42nd Street. Originally illuminated
with incandescent bulbs, in 1939
Claude Neon Lights retrofitted one
of the two signs with neon tubes
in "fluorescent old gold." (The
other sign probably disappeared at
this time.) In 1995 the building's
owners proposed the sign's
removal but were rebuffed by a
unanimous vote by the Landmarks
Preservation Commission.

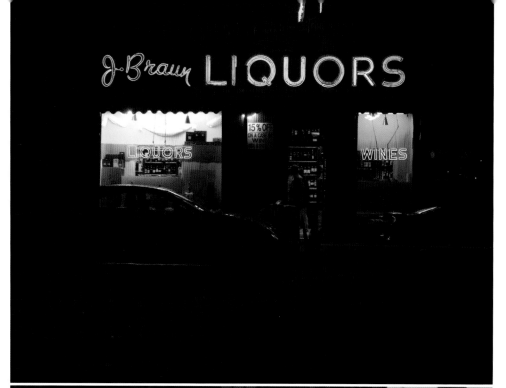

## UPTOWN LIQUORS (FORMERLY JULIUS BRAUN LIQUORS)

1361 Lexington Avenue, 1952, union sign shop no. 17

The same shop that produced the great sign of the P&G Bar (see page 99) made this appealing fascia display for Julius Braun Liquors in 1952.

## WAVERLY RESTAURANT

11 Waverly Place, c. 1959*

The Waverly Restaurant's triptych of neon fascia and swing signs made way for new signs styled after their predecessors (shown here) in 2008.

## VENIERO PASTICCERIA

342 East 11th Street, c. 1945

Antonio Veniero opened this east side pasticceria in 1894 after emigrating to New York from a small town on the Bay of Naples. His descendants continue to run the business more than a century later. The shop's unique projecting sign dates to the years immediately following World War II.

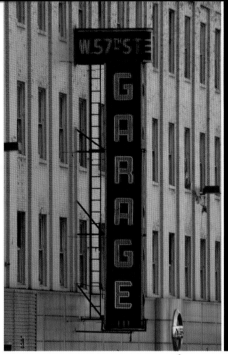

## WEST 43RD STREET GARAGE

249 West 43rd Street,
1950

Tail-finned Cadillacs once found refuge from the clamor of Times Square at the West 43rd Street Garage, opened around 1949. Sandwiched between the old Times Square Hotel and the former home of the *New York Times*, the building's most remarkable feature has always been its enormous vertical neon display. To hold its own in such close proximity to the Times Square spectaculars a block away (which at the time of its installation included the famous smoke ring–puffing Camel Cigarettes sign), this display originally featured an animated illumination sequence in which its letters flashed on and off in alternating hues of red and green. Today, only the red tubes remain. It makes a very brief cameo in Gordon Parks's 1971 film *Shaft*.

## WEST 57TH STREET GARAGE

622 West 57th Street, 1949,
E. G. Clarke Inc.

Streamlined stainless-steel moldings lend distinction to this large vertical sign, which recalls the days when the Atlantic liners of the Swedish American Line tied up a stone's throw away at the foot of West 57th Street. Its maker, E. G. Clarke Inc., was among New York's most prominent electric sign shops even before neon came on the scene in 1924.

## WHITE HORSE TAVERN

567 Hudson Street, 1946,
Allen Sign Co.

Opened in 1880, the White Horse spent its first seventy-five years as a fairly ordinary neighborhood bar. By the 1950s it became a haunt for a cast of well-known bohemians, including Allen Ginsberg, Jack Kerouac, and, perhaps most famously, Dylan Thomas, who all came here to liquefy their royalties. It has remained more or less frozen in time since then, though its bohemian denizens have mostly decamped to more affordable climes.

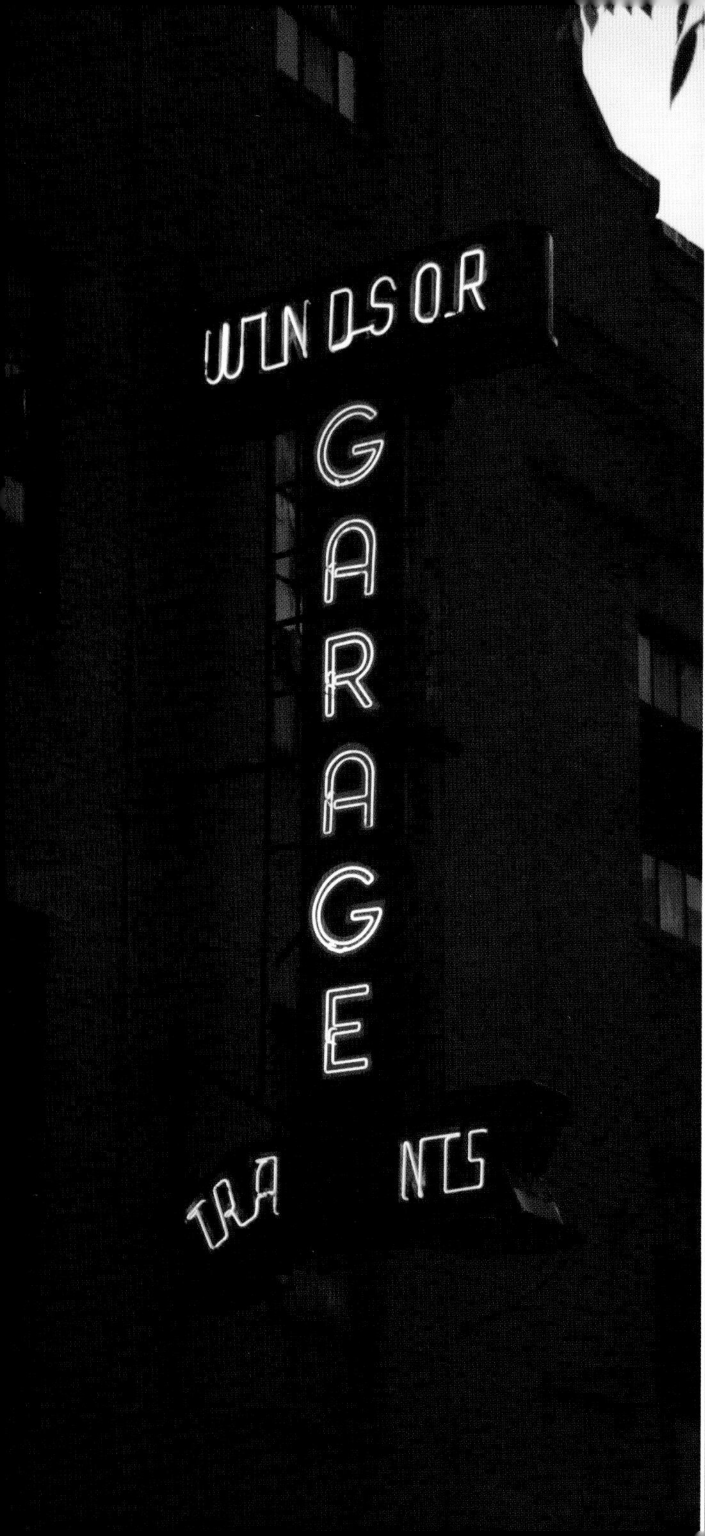
WINDSOR
GARAGE
TRA
NTS

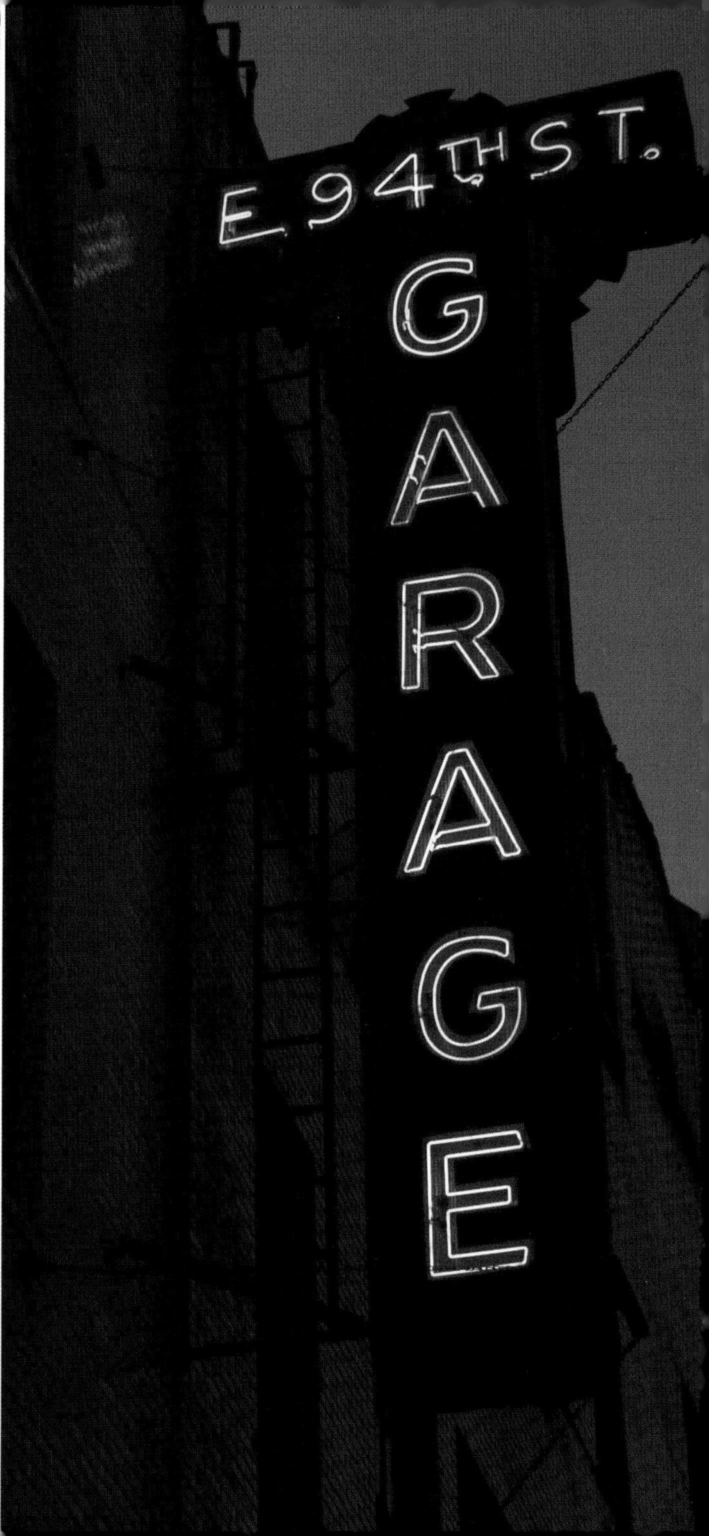
E. 94TH ST.
GARAGE

 ⇦

## WINDSOR GARAGE

332 East 76th Street, 1947

One of the more endearing aspects of old neon signs is their outdated use of certain vernacular terms. When the Windsor Garage installed this pleasing vertical display in 1947, the word "transient" carried rather different connotations than it does today.

⇦

## YORKVILLE GARAGE

231 East 94th Street, c. 1937*

Manhattan parking garages began installing electric signs at an early date: New York Edison tallied up nearly one thousand "auto and garage" displays in Manhattan as early as 1927. With dependability rather than high fashion a factor in their trade, garages have apparently felt less compelled than other businesses to update their signage. As a result, these establishments retain some of Manhattan's finest examples of vintage neon today, such as this especially handsome example on the Upper East Side.

## WONG'S CHINESE

2341 Adam Clayton Powell Boulevard, 1937

This former chow mein and chop suey joint occupied part of the former Renaissance Theatre and Casino in Harlem. Built in two phases in 1921 and 1923, the Renaissance complex closed in 1979, and the building has decayed since then. The Landmarks Commission declined to include the property on its list of protected historic sites in 2007, and the sign vanished with the partial demolition of the building behind it in 2010. In its evocative, forlorn state, the old marquee was ripe for comparison with another faded sign, depicted in Edward Hopper's *Chop Suey* of 1929.

## LOUIS ZUFLACHT "SMART CLOTHES"

154 Stanton Street, 1942

Louis Zuflacht, a Lower East Side purveyor of "smart clothes," unfortunately did not survive to benefit from the notoriety of his ghost sign, now one of the area's favorite vestigial landmarks. Installed in 1942, this was one of the last neon signs made in New York before World War II forced the city's neon sign shops into a three-year hiatus. The storefront has lately housed an art gallery.

THE SIGNS

# THE BRONX

## EGIDIO PASTRY SHOP

622 East 187th Street, c. 1967*

The Belmont section of the Bronx retains a strong Italian-American identity thanks to a concentration of old neighborhood institutions such as this, which has operated continuously since 1912.

## FRANK'S SPORT SHOP

430 East Tremont Avenue, 1949

Frank Stein opened this sporting goods and army-navy store circa 1921. The neon sign came later, in 1949. The business eventually passed to Frank's son, Moe, whom the *New York Times* called "as much an institution as his store."

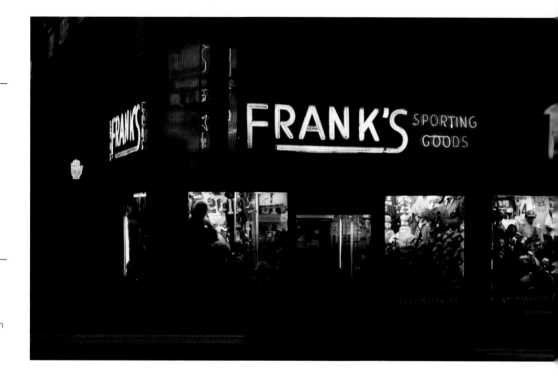

## LOEW'S PARADISE THEATRE

2403 Grand Concourse, 1929;
Strauss Sign Co. & Claude Neon
Lights, Inc.?

The immense neon fascia sign of the Loew's Paradise Theatre is original to the building's opening in 1929, making it possibly the earliest functioning neon display in the five boroughs. Restrictive sign ordinances prohibiting marquees and projecting signs along the Grand Concourse account for its unusual arrangement, in being flush with the facade. The building is the work of the prolific movie-house designer John Eberson, who also drew plans for the former Earle Theatre in Jackson Heights, Queens (see page 165). With seating for more than three thousand, the Paradise belongs to a set of five movie palaces known as Loew's "Wonder Theatres," which opened in the New York area in 1929–1930. The theater and its sign were both restored in the 2000s after a period of abandonment.

## LOEW'S POST ROAD THEATRE
3475 Boston Road, 1939,
Artkraft Strauss Sign Corp.

Opened in 1939, the former Loew's Post Road is among the last of nearly two hundred theaters designed by the architect Thomas W. Lamb. Its gracefully streamlined upright sign is the work of Artkraft Strauss, whose predecessor, the Strauss Sign Company, secured contracts to handle nearly all outdoor signs and marquees for Loew's New York–area theaters in the 1920s. Originally lettered to read LOEW'S, the sign was subsequently re-lettered when the theater changed ownership. Various factors caused the great majority of New York's old neighborhood movie theaters to close in the 1960s and 1970s. The Post Road later housed a Baptist Church and, more recently, a supermarket.

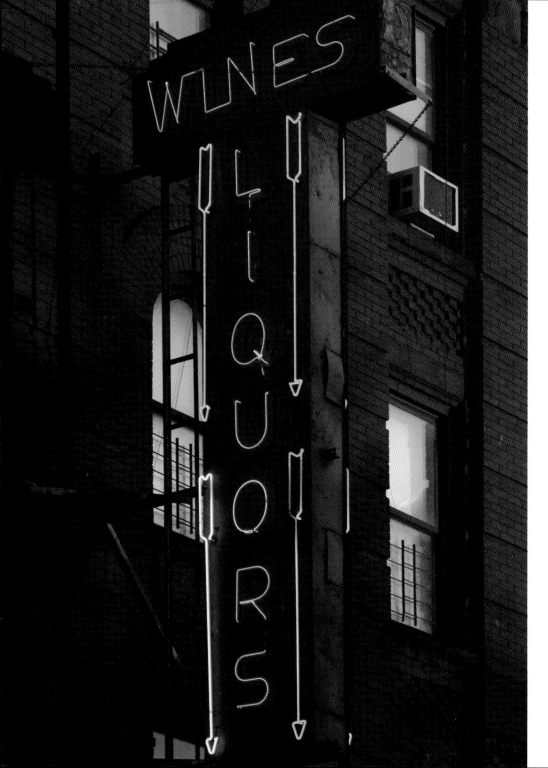

## WILLIS WINES AND LIQUORS

222 Willis Avenue, c. 1934*

Housing projects directly across the street from this early neon sign testify to the vast changes that have swept the South Bronx since this display made its appearance here circa 1934. The sign's weathered faces are especially appealing set against the warm brick facades of the nineteenth-century tenements beyond. It offers a rare surviving example of the "raised letter" typology that went extinct before World War II.

## PALOMBA ACADEMY OF MUSIC

974 East Gun Hill Road, 1956, Grauer Sign Co.

Manhattan had New York's original Academy of Music, Fort Greene still has the Brooklyn Academy of Music, and East Gun Hill Road has the Palomba Academy of Music, in business for more than fifty years.

THE SIGNS
# BROOKLYN

## ANTELIS PHARMACY

1502 Elm Avenue, c. 1955,
Silverescent Neon Sign Co.*

The Silverescent Neon Sign Co.'s
longtime layout man, Charlie Klein,
devised a handsome formula for the
design of neighborhood drugstore
signs that the firm deployed
with slight variations throughout
Brooklyn in the 1950s. One of these
survives over the storefront of the
Antelis Pharmacy on Elm Avenue in
Midwood, still in remarkably good
order after nearly six decades of
continuous service.

## BAY RIDGE
## ANIMAL HOSPITAL

6803 Fifth Avenue, c. 1950,
Higger Sign Co.

There was no limit to the range
of businesses that advertised
with neon during the midcentury
decades, as this simple but pleasing
vertical sign attests.

## BOULEVARD TAVERN

575 Meeker Ave., c. 1935

Very handsome "thick-and-thin" lettering adds charm to this swing sign in Greenpoint, Brooklyn. Such letterforms became a hackneyed point of reference for nostalgic evocations of prewar New York in the 1970s and 1980s, lending authentic examples (like that seen here) an added appeal.

## BRUNO TRUCK SALES

435 Hamilton Avenue, c. 1965

This is the most recent of three on-premise spectaculars in the Gowanus section of Brooklyn, positioned to catch the eye of motorists on the adjacent Gowanus Expressway.

## THE CYCLONE

834 Surf Avenue, c. 1950

Opened in 1927, the Cyclone is
the best known and last of three
large wood-track roller coasters
that operated contemporaneously
at Coney Island through much of
the twentieth century. Its existing
neon vertical display replaced a
similarly proportioned incandescent
bulb sign around the year 1950.
The Landmarks Preservation
Commission declared the structure
a protected historic site in 1988.

## CHENG'S CHINESE RESTAURANT

823 Nostrand Avenue, c. 1953*,
Royal Neon Signs

Chinese restaurants exhibited a
particular affinity for electric signs
even before neon first appeared
in New York in the 1920s. Joseph
Mitchell described Chinatown as a
"galaxy of neon signs" in 1940. The
trend reached far beyond the Lower
East Side of Manhattan: this sign
has long outlived the restaurant it
advertised in the Crown Heights
section of Brooklyn.

## CIRCO'S PASTRY SHOP

312 Knickerbocker Avenue,
c. 1953*

Circo Pastry Shop's particularly
handsome neon fascia and vertical
signs mark this as one of the very
few old businesses that have
survived dramatic demographic
shifts in this neighborhood during
the past half-century.

# DENO'S WONDER WHEEL AMUSEMENT PARK

3059 West 12th Street,
c. 1930, c. 1950

A small army of neon (and incandescent bulb) signs advertise Coney Island's famed Wonder Wheel, built by the aptly named Eccentric Ferris Wheel Co. in 1920. Most of the Wonder Wheel's signs are of midcentury vintage. One, standing modestly beneath the wheel off to one side, likely dates to the late 1920s, making it possibly the oldest neon display in New York.

## M. DEVITO PAINT AND WALLCOVERING
371 Graham Avenue, c. 1955,
Silverescent Neon Sign Co.?

This vertical sign showcases
the development of fluorescent
coatings for luminous tubes.
Introduced in 1933, fluorescent
coatings increased the neon sign
maker's palette from a small
handful of luminous hues to an
almost unlimited color range.

## EAGLE CLOTHES
213 Sixth Street, 1951,
White Way Neon Sign Co.

Perched atop an unadorned
warehouse, the great roof sign
of this defunct men's clothier has
been a fixture on the Brooklyn
skyline for six decades. Eagle
prospered in an era when men
typically wore jackets and ties
to even the most casual of
engagements, contributing in its
way to the midcentury aesthetic
of the city. Like the nearby Kentile
Floors spectacular (see page 150),
the Eagle display was "strategically
placed to attract the attention of an
estimated 170,000 people a day"
who passed by on the nearby IND
subway and Gowanus Expressway,
according to a November 1951
story in *Signs of the Times*. The
sign originally featured a "realistic
back-lighted skyline silhouette
of plastic buildings" over the
globe, now gone. Mayor Vincent
Impelleteri presided over the
plant's ribbon cutting in 1951. Eagle
survived until declaring bankruptcy
in 1989.

## FABER'S ARCADE

1230 Surf Avenue, c. 1948*,
Silverescent Neon Sign Corp.

For more than sixty years, this
large fascia sign (part of a trio)
hung over the entrance to Faber's
Arcade. Faber's had occupied part
of the former Henderson's Music
Hall building from the 1930s until
the site was cleared as part of an
unpopular redevelopment scheme
in 2010–2011, despite pleas for
its preservation by community
activists. Once more common,
"fascination" signs typically
identified midway-type amusement
arcades. Similar signs could be
found in Times Square into the
1970s, receiving less-than-flattering
depictions in John Rechy's novel
*City of Night* and Martin Scorsese's
film *Taxi Driver*. Faber's signs
survived long enough to earn a
nostalgic appeal. Designed by the
Silverescent Neon Sign Corp.'s
veteran layout man, Charles Klein,
the display eventually lost its
neon tubes, but its "scintillating"
incandescent bulbs remained
functional until the sign was
dismantled in 2010.

## FARRELL'S BAR & GRILL

215 Prospect Park West, c. 1935*
(facsimile by Paul Signs Inc., 2011)

Farrell's original neon sign hung over the entrance to this neighborhood bar from around 1935 until a winter storm sent it crashing to the sidewalk in December 2010. The existing display (pictured) is a convincing facsimile by Paul Signs of Brooklyn, which also restored the original sign for installation within the bar. The new sign carries over the distinctive silhouette and raised sheet metal letters of the original.

## GARRY JEWELERS

474 Fifth Avenue, c. 1955

This is among several surviving displays that recall a trend in sign design that exploited the eye-catching contrast between elegant scripts and sans-serif grotesque letterforms, which peaked in the early to mid-1950s.

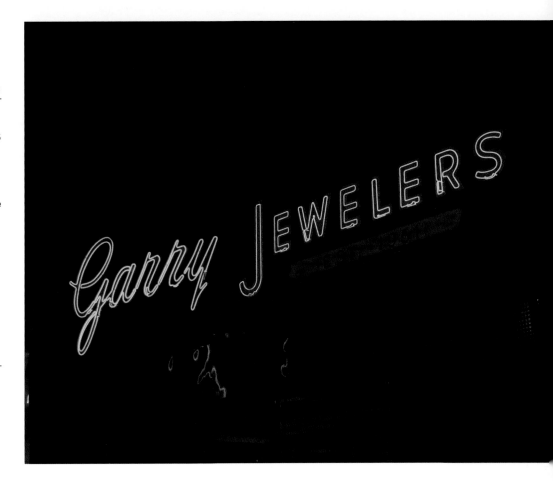

## HAROLD'S
## PHARMACY

2272 McDonald Avenue, c. 1955,
Super Neon Light Inc.

Elongated neon fascia signs on two
elevations brighten this corner under
the elevated tracks of the Culver Line
of the IND subway. The signs are
the work of Super Neon Light Inc.,
whose displays have characterized
the storefronts of this and other
Brooklyn neighborhoods for decades.

## HINSCH'S
## CONFECTIONARY

8518 Fifth Avenue,
c. 1948

Hinsch's soda fountain and
luncheonette originally operated
on 18th Avenue in Brooklyn, and it
moved to its current location in 1948.
The signs likely date from that year.
The storefront previously belonged to
a confectionary called Reichert's.

## KATZ
## DRUGS

76 Graham Avenue, c. 1955,
Silverescent Neon Sign Co.

Many who gush at the sight of
this three-story extravaganza of
neon, stainless steel, and porcelain
enamel would wince at the thought
of slathering such a creation over
a historic nineteenth-century
facade today.

## KENTILE FLOORS

58 Second Avenue, c. 1954,
White Way Neon Sign Co.

Kentile, a defunct maker of floor
tiles, is known in legal circles as
the subject of asbestos litigation.
In Brooklyn the company is better
known as the patron of this sign,
which stands by the Gowanus
Canal. It is the most prominent
of three surviving on-premise
spectaculars built to catch the
attention of passengers on the
adjacent above-ground stretch of
the IND crosstown subway and of
motorists on the nearby Gowanus
Expressway. A visit to online photo-
sharing websites reveals the Kentile
sign's immense popularity among
amateur photographers today. In
2010, New York's Municipal Art
Society added the Kentile display
to its list of "Places That Matter."
The sign has a near twin atop
another former Kentile plant in
Chicago, Illinois.

## KINGSTON LOUNGE

120 Kingston Avenue, c. 1947*

The forlorn facade of this former
nightclub in Crown Heights,
Brooklyn, retains its bold good
looks despite years of neglect. Its
distinctive juxtaposition of red and
black structural glass with neon and
stainless steel must have made a
fine sight with neon tubes aglow
at dusk.

## M&M PHARMACY

1901 Avenue M, c. 1945

Bright neon tubes outlining especially appealing midcentury letterforms are set against a backdrop of black Carrara glass, making this one of Brooklyn's more distinctive period storefronts.

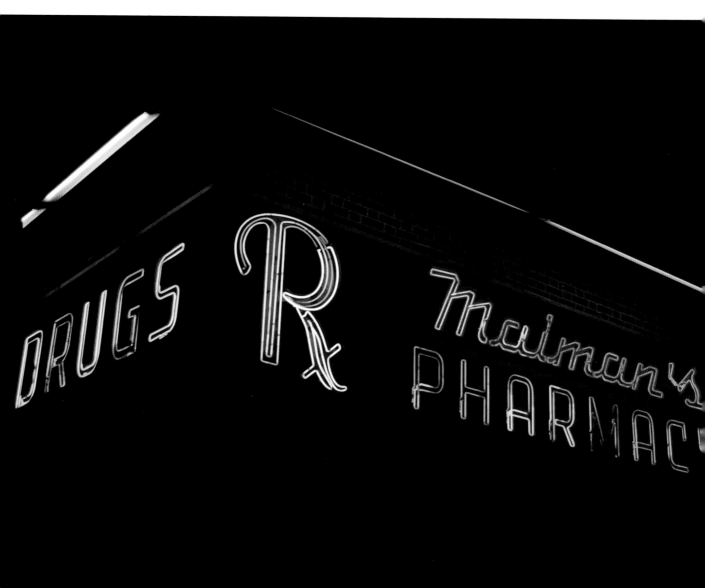

## MAIMAN'S
## PHARMACY

821 Franklin Avenue, c. 1951*,
Silverescent Neon Sign Co.

Along with the sign advertising the Antelis Pharmacy (see page 134), this display exemplified a more-or-less standard design for small neighborhood drugstores, created by Silverescent's longtime layout man, Charles Klein, in the 1950s. Maiman's survived good times and bad on the corner of Franklin Avenue and Eastern Parkway in Crown Heights, until it finally closed and the sign was removed in 2012.

## MONTERO
## BAR AND GRILL
**73 Atlantic Avenue, c. 1949\*,**
**Corvin Neon Lights**

Just two blocks from the place
where Atlantic Avenue meets the
sea, Montero's merchant marine
décor is living testimony to a time
when "the New York port" was
the city's very reason for being.
The bar's streamlined neon sign is
still visible from the foot of Atlantic
Avenue, but these days most
of its customers come from the
other direction.

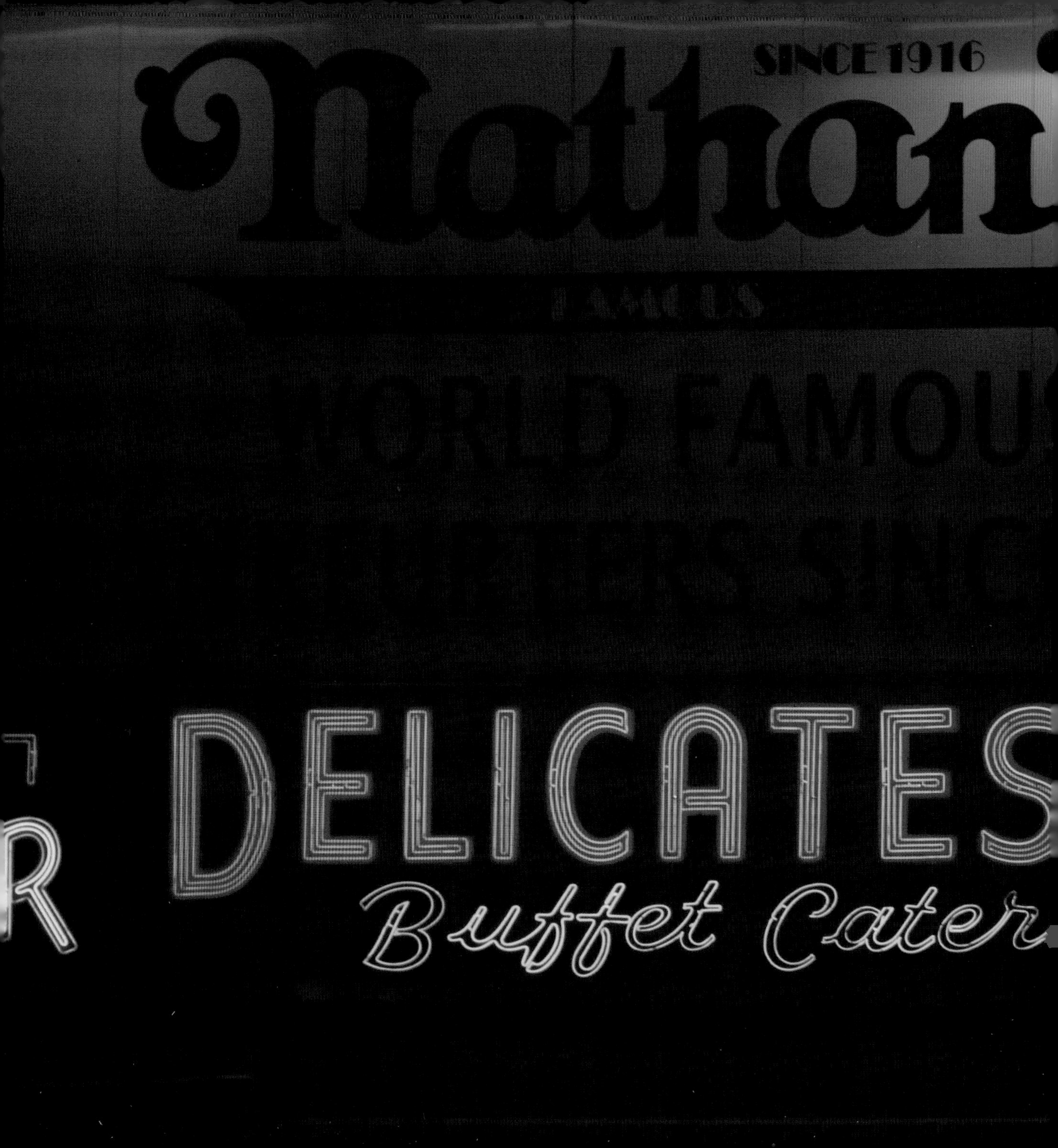
SINCE 1916
Nathan
ORLD FAMOU
DELICATES
Buffet Cater

ORIGINAL
NATHANS
Nathan's
FAMOUS INC.
TAKE
FOOD
FAMOUS
FRANKFURTERS
SEN

## NATHAN'S FAMOUS INC.

1310 Surf Avenue, c. 1930
(vertical), c. 1960*, Salzman
Sign Co. (projecting and fascia)

Nathan Handwerk opened his
first frankfurter stand at Coney
Island in 1916, and the operation
eventually grew to become a
nationwide chain. The company's
flagship location today boasts the
best surviving display of historic
neon advertising anywhere in the
five boroughs. The signs date from
two periods: the vertical display,
installed circa 1930, is one of New
York's oldest functioning neon
signs. The others came about thirty
years later, the work of the Salzman
Sign Co., for many years a Brooklyn
institution in its own right.

## NEERGAARD PHARMACY

454 Fifth Avenue, c. 1950,
Silverescent Neon Sign Co.

Neergaard's has operated from this
location since 1888. The existing
sign appeared after World War II,
replacing an earlier display of similar
configuration. Copy reading OPEN
24 HOURS is a recent addition,
though Neergaard's has held down
this round-the-clock schedule for
more than ninety years.

## O'KEEFE'S BAR AND GRILL

62 Court Street,
c. 1946*

This sign was originally installed for the Savoy Bar and Grill at 355 West 41st Street in Manhattan around 1946, and moved to its current residence in downtown Brooklyn about fifty years later.

## QUEEN MARIE ITALIAN RESTAURANT

84 Court Street, 1961

Anthony Vitiello opened this restaurant at 98 Court Street in 1958 after coming to New York from Torra del Greco, near Naples, Italy. The sign appeared three years later, when the restaurant expanded. When the business moved to a new storefront down the street three decades later, the fascia sign came with it. Mr. Vitiello's sons continue to manage the family business today.

## VASIKAUSKAS BAR AND GRILL

279 Grand Street,
c. 1950*

The fascia sign of the Vasikauskas Bar and Grill juxtaposes blackletter and grotesque lettering to pleasing effect on Grand Street in Williamsburg.

## WASHINGTON TEMPLE CHURCH OF GOD IN CHRIST

1372 Bedford Avenue,
c. 1956*

New York's greatest display of sacred neon belongs to the Washington Temple Church, facing out over Grant Square in Crown Heights. The building claims several noteworthy distinctions: built as a vaudeville theater around 1906, it later became a movie house, reopening as the Loews Bedford Theatre in the 1920s. Later still it became one of many New York theaters to find new use as a house of worship. It is said to have witnessed the public debuts of entertainer Fanny Brice and of the Reverend Al Sharpton, who read his first sermon here in 1959, at age four. The sign is generally only lit for services.

## WATCHTOWER BIBLE AND TRACT SOCIETY

51 Furman Street,
c. 1969

The sturdy, reinforced concrete warehouses beneath this sign once belonged to the pharmaceuticals manufacturer E. R. Squibb and Sons, whose industrial compound occupied the Brooklyn Heights waterfront for more than a century beginning in 1856. Squibb's large roof sign remained a familiar skyline sight for many years. The Watchtower Bible and Tract Society, better known as Jehovah's Witnesses, moved into the buildings in 1969 and erected this sign in place of Squibb's, availing themselves of a grandfather clause in zoning ordinances that effectively outlawed large illuminated roof signs.

## WYCKOFF PAINT FAIR

146 Wyckoff Avenue,
c. 1950

Its neon tubes are gone, but this vertical sign carries on over Wyckoff Avenue in Bushwick.

## WILLIAMSBURGH SAVINGS BANK TOWER

One Hanson Place, 1929,
Claude Neon Lights Inc.

Designed by the architects Halsey, McCormack & Helmer, the Williamsburgh Savings Bank Tower boasted many superlatives upon its completion in 1929: it was not only the tallest building in Brooklyn, but was also sometimes described as the "tallest skyscraper between Manhattan and Paris." Claude Neon proudly featured the building in its monthly newsletter, noting that the tower featured "the largest four-faced illuminated clock in the world," whose twelve- and seventeen-foot neon hands could be seen for miles around. Recently restored, the great neon clock may be the last working installation originally created by Georges Claude's original New York sign shop.

THE SIGNS
# QUEENS

# JOE ABBRACCIAMENTO RESTAURANT

62–96 Woodhaven Boulevard, c. 1949, New York Neon (alterations, c. 1998 by Artistic Neon Inc.)

Three signs from three periods advertise this Italian restaurant in Rego Park. The "Abbracciamento" sign dates to around 1949, when the business operated on Cross Bay Boulevard. About a year later the restaurant moved to its current location and took the sign with them. "Catering" and "Restaurant" are later additions, installed around 1980 and 1998, respectively.

# AIR LINE DINER

63–95 Astoria Boulevard, c. 1952

Built in 1952 by the Mountain View Diner Co. of Singac, New Jersey, the Air Line took its name because of its proximity to LaGuardia Field (opened as the New York Municipal Airport in 1939 and officially renamed for the charismatic New York mayor in 1947). In recent years the Air Line has been operated as part of the Jackson Hole chain, which augmented the diner's original neon displays with new signs in the spirit of the existing ones. It makes a cameo in Martin Scorsese's 1990 film *Goodfellas*.

## BROADWAY WINE AND LIQUOR

38—09 Broadway, c. 1945

Neon signs bedecked this stretch of Broadway in Astoria by the 1930s, but almost none have survived to the twenty-first century. Curved porcelain-enamel panels and moderne thick-and-thin lettering make this stand out as one of the better period storefronts anywhere in the five boroughs today.

## BERNARD F. DOWD FUNERAL HOME INC.

165-20 Hillside Avenue, c. 1955*,
Grauer Sign Co. (alterations,
c. 1982 by Grauer Sign Co.)

Sedate neon script in white marks the spot of the Bernard F. Dowd Funeral Home in Jamaica. "Although it carries a theme suggesting gayety or festivity in its usual form, there is always an underlying quality of beauty and charm in its colors that evokes an appreciative response from us—not unlike one's appreciation of flowers or of an orchard in bloom," wrote a sign designer named Peter Horsley of neon in an article entitled "Neon for the Funeral Home" (published in the September 1950 issue of *Signs of the Times*). "If this quality can be recognized separately from the blatancy of the illumination, and the colors used tastefully, neon may carve a wider niche in the advertising schemes of establishments such as religious institutions, church supply houses, funeral parlors and the like."

## EAGLE THEATER

73–03 37th Road, c. 1939

This streamlined marquee complemented the moderne styling of the building from which it hung. The theater (and possibly the marquee) is the work of the architect John Eberson, who designed dozens of cinemas across the United States. Eberson's other works include two of the enormous Loew's "Wonder Theatres," including the Loew's Paradise in the Bronx (page 130). The Earle was a more modest neighborhood theater, built after the fussy plaster ornament of the movie palace era had fallen from favor. When moviegoing itself fell out of favor, the Earle landed on tough times, eventually resorting to adult films to stay afloat. It later reopened as the "Eagle," a Bollywood theater catering to Jackson Heights's growing Indian community until it shuttered again in 2009. The marquee was removed in 2012.

## ESTATES DRUG CO.

169–01 Hillside Avenue, c. 1940

Jamaica, Queens, boasted one of New York's finest examples of moderne storefront architecture until an unfortunate remodeling did away with the sleek, understated facade of the Estates pharmacy in 2010.

## EDDIE'S SWEET SHOP

105–29 Metropolitan Avenue, c. 1950*

Known as Eddie's Sweet Shop since 1968, this corner ice cream parlor opened much earlier, around the time of the Versailles Treaty. Strategically positioned near a neighborhood movie theater, Eddie's sells ice cream made on the premises.

## EDWARD D. LYNCH FUNERAL HOME

43—07 Queens Boulevard, c. 1948*, Serota Sign Corp.?

This funeral parlor opened in 1931. Like neon signs for churches, luminous tube funeral-home displays are reminders of a time before the popular psyche's association of neon with less solemn enterprises came about during the 1950s and 1960s. Undertakers and funeral directors began using electric signs well before the arrival of neon. Sign surveys conducted by New York Edison found forty-two electric signs for funeral homes in Manhattan (below 135th Street) by 1927.

## NEW PARK PIZZA

156–71 Cross Bay Boulevard, c. 1960, LaSalle Sign Corp.

New Park Pizza is a neighborhood institution of the first order, family owned and operated since it opened here in 1955.

⇧

## PEPSI-COLA

Long Island City, 1936,
Artkraft Strauss Sign Corp.

For nearly seventy years, Long Island City's signature Pepsi spectacular stood on the roof of a Pepsi-Cola bottling plant that occupied a nearby stretch of the East River waterfront. The plant made way for residential high-rises in 2004–2005, but the sign has survived. It was first re-erected on terra-firma near its original location, then moved again slightly to the north in 2008. The Landmarks Commission considered extending protective designation to the sign in 1988 but took no action. Artkraft Strauss, the sign's original fabricator, completely refurbished the display in 1994, replacing much of its original sheet metal fabric. On-premise spectaculars positioned over waterfront industrial buildings once were a characteristic scene of New York Harbor, but they have gone the way of steam ferries and Atlantic liners since zoning regulations effectively outlawed their construction in the 1960s.

## THE QUAYS PUB (FORMERLY COFFEY'S CORNER CAFÉ)

45–02 30th Avenue, Astoria,
c. 1951*

Green neon tubes herald this
comfortable Irish pub in Astoria.
The sign is a relic from Coffey's
Corner Café, which previously
occupied this storefront.

## QUEENS LIQUOR AND WINE STORE

59–03 Myrtle Avenue, c. 1948
(vertical), c. 1968 (fascia)

One of New York's more lavish
liquor store displays adorns the
storefront of the Queens Liquor and
Wine Store on Myrtle Avenue in
Ridgewood. The fascia sign made
its debut at a time when many
shop owners began to abandon
traditional neon displays in favor of
cheaper alternatives.

## UNITED AIRLINES

LaGuardia Airport, c. 1960,
Midtown Neon Sign Co.

This elegant display at LaGuardia
Airport recalls the logotype used
by United Airlines for its aircraft
livery and promotional literature
from 1954 until the mid-1960s.
It is a small miracle that the sign
has managed to evade several
generations of updated corporate
identity schemes.

⇧

# SILVERCUP STUDIOS (FORMERLY SILVERCUP BAKERY)

42—22 22nd Street, c. 1961–62,
Artkraft Strauss Sign Corp.

Silvercup Studios moved into the former Silvercup Bakery in 1983. Since then, this facility has been used for an incredibly long list of film and television productions. The enormous roof sign survives from the structure's previous livelihood, having been altered only with the substitution of the word STUDIOS for BAKERY at the bottom center and with the loss of its neon tubes (the sign is floodlit now). Once upon a time, Long Island City hosted what may have been New York's greatest concentration of on-premise spectaculars, which beamed out from atop the area's industrial lofts. Some, like the signs for Silvercup and Pepsi-Cola, aimed their messages across the East River toward Manhattan. But most, including those over the Executone intercom and Swingline stapler factories, shone out over the Sunnyside railroad yards, targeting commuters riding the Long Island Rail Road.

THE SIGNS
# STATEN ISLAND

## DELCO DRUGS AND SPECIALTY PHARMACY AND LENNY'S CLEANERS (FORMERLY EMPIRE CLEANERS)

3833 Richmond Ave., Eltingville, c. 1965, Neon Eagle Sign Corp.

This matched set of elegant neon signs has marked the spot of Delco Drugs and Lenny's Cleaners in the southern Staten Island community of Eltingville since about 1965, making them contemporaries of another Staten Island landmark, the Verrazano-Narrows Bridge. The bridge has made a significant impact on Staten Island's landscape, if indirectly: the borough's population more than doubled to half a million residents in the five decades since it opened. Lenny's and Delco have survived the upheaval and offer two of the island's more appealing storefronts more than four decades later.

## MILLER'S PRESCRIPTIONS

173 Broad Street, Stapleton, c. 1958*

Opened by Alfred Miller shortly after World War II, this neighborhood drug store originally occupied a storefront across the street from its present location. Displaced by urban renewal redevelopment, the business moved to its current address in the late 1950s. The sign dates from this period.

## ELTINGVILLE PHARMACY

3948 Richmond Avenue, Eltingville,
c. 1961, Torrone Signs

This neon fascia sign crowns the entrance of a neighborhood drug store situated in a small strip mall. Like many signs from the midcentury decades, it plays on the stark juxtaposition of elegant script and bold, sans-serif block lettering. "Before the advent of modern logo design, scripts gave the illusion that the business name was a signature," Steven Heller and Louise Fili wrote in their book *Scripts: Elegant Lettering from Design's Golden Age.* "They made the impersonal personal."

RMACY

# PRESERVING HISTORIC SIGNS

Much of the appeal of historic neon signs owes to the sense of authenticity exuded by their "accidental" survival in the landscape. However, as increasingly rare works of vernacular design that are significant in their own right, many historic signs (neon and otherwise) warrant active initiatives to ensure their survival when they inevitably reach the end of their service lives. Across the United States, various governmental and nonprofit entities have taken steps to identify, document, and preserve neon and other historic signs. To date, almost no such action has taken place in New York City, leaving this important element of our built heritage largely undocumented in the place where commercial electric signs were born.

Like other landmarks, historic signs are of greatest value when they are in their original environs. In Los Angeles, a unique public–private partnership cleverly christened the Living Urban Museum of Electric and Neon Signs (LUMENS) project has established a successful model for the conservation of historic neon signs in place. The initiative was launched in 1998 as a joint venture of the city's Department of Cultural Affairs and the Los Angeles–based Museum of Neon Art. It has channeled both public and private funds toward the restoration of numerous historic neon signs in cooperation with property owners. The Museum of Neon Art organizes nighttime tours to view the restored signs. Los Angeles's fair climate lends an extra advantage toward any effort to preserve neon signs outdoors, and indeed it has played no small role in leaving the city with so many historic signs to preserve.

But even with a fair-weather advantage, the preservation of historic signs in outdoor locations faces myriad practical limitations that render any such program extremely complicated to administer and enforce. A more common solution has been to preserve historic signs indoors, within museums and private collections. The Museum of Neon Art is one of at least three dedicated sign museums that have opened in the United States since 1981, having been followed by the Neon Museum in Las Vegas (opened in 1996) and the American Sign Museum in Cincinnati (opened in 2005). Other museums, such as the Smithsonian National Museum of American History in Washington, D.C., and the Henry Ford Museum in Dearborn, Michigan, have also actively collected historic neon and other types of signs.

In New York, a city whose relationship with electric signs has been a definitive part of its twentieth-century identity, there is no formal program to document, preserve, or encourage the conservation of historic signs. Of more than 100,000 electric signs installed in Manhattan between 1916 and 1960, only one has found its way into the collection of a museum dedicated to the city's history. A handful of others, such as the sign that once advertised Ratner's kosher

ABOVE and OPPOSITE Publicity photos showing New York installations of Claude Neon Lights, Inc., and its successor firm, the Serota Sign Corp., between the 1930s and 1950s. Signs like these, which characterized streetscapes throughout the city, have vanished with little or no documentation.

restaurant on East Houston Street, have been preserved in private collections. The rest have been left to their fate. A survey conducted for this book in 2010 found about four hundred neon signs from the period between 1930 and 1965 still in place throughout the five boroughs. However, the total number has diminished significantly since I began research in 2006.

A number of steps can be taken to preserve the signs or record them for future study. Their highly ephemeral nature and complex legal relationships with the buildings from which they hang have challenged the ability of New York's Landmarks Preservation Commission to protect the signs with landmark designations. So far, not one sign in New York has been designated as a protected landmark in its own right. The commission could develop a policy to guide its approach toward this issue. Short of creating a citywide survey of historic signs and identifying candidates for designation, the agency could more clearly establish the parameters of its legal powers to protect signs as integral parts of historic storefronts. It could more closely scrutinize the replication of historic signs in order to consider details such as finish materials and color.

But even if historic signs could be kept in place by legal decree, there would still come a time when these perishable objects would

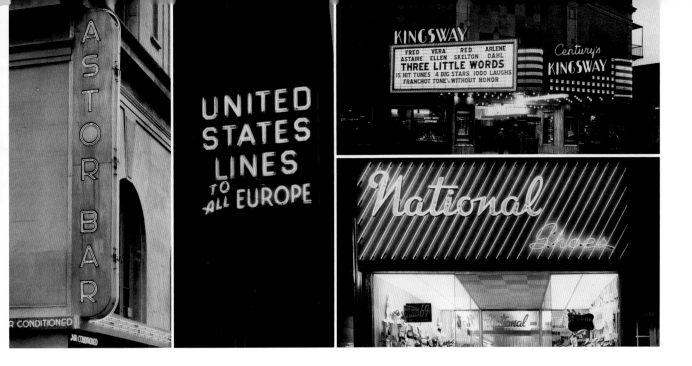

require careful restoration or replication. Their conservation in perpetuity would ultimately require moving them to the protection of an indoor environment, with replicas installed in their place. A small nonprofit could set about identifying historic signs and raising funds to provide for their maintenance and stewardship, both outdoors and in. Such an organization could open a small museum of signs, or it could help raise an endowment to enable existing cultural institutions to take more historic signs under their wings.

The initiatives described above would require the allocation of time, money, and real estate, none of which has thus far been forthcoming. If conserving the signs themselves proves infeasible, then formal efforts to document them in drawings and photographs and to gather and archive records related to the sign industry may be practical alternatives. This book is a step in that direction. The Smithsonian Institution and the New York Public Library have conserved archival materials of Douglas Leigh and the Artkraft Strauss Sign Corporation, respectively, thus preserving a record of the famous off-premise spectaculars of Times Square. But the significance of documents related to the more pervasive and arguably more significant on-premise storefront signs has yet to receive such recognition.

The work of New York's small sign shops continues to have a tremendous impact on our experience of the city. Neon signs of the early and middle decades of the twentieth century are the highest-quality remains of the collective work by skilled sign painters and designers, sheet metal workers, tube benders, and electricians. Though signs are ephemeral by nature, significant numbers of neon signs from this period remain in service six, seven, and even eight decades after their installations, setting an endurance record that (at least in New York) has exceeded that of the traditional signs they replaced, and that is unlikely to be matched by the signs that have succeeded them. Historically, these virtues have often been lost in the mix of our fraught relationship with neon signs. But their enduring ability to stir strong feelings is a testament to the significance of neon signs as works of design and as objects of cultural heritage.

## ARTKRAFT STRAUSS SIGN CORP.

Artkraft Strauss formed in 1936 from the merger of Strauss & Co. (founded in New York in 1897) and of the New York arm of the Artkraft Sign Company, based in Lima, Ohio. In the 1920s, Strauss had the distinction of being possibly the first American sign company to enter into a franchise agreement with Claude Neon. The merger of Strauss and Artkraft was orchestrated by Jacob Starr, a Jewish immigrant who had arrived in New York from what is now Ukraine in 1907; Starr subsequently took control of the new company. Working collaboratively with the outdoor advertising promoter Douglas Leigh, Artkraft Strauss managed to oust the General Outdoor Advertising Company as the leading creator of the off-premise spectaculars of Times Square and elsewhere by the late 1930s, a position it held until the 1990s. From the 1930s until the company discontinued its sign making and maintenance operations in 2006, its plant occupied a former garage building at Twelfth Avenue and West 57th Street, adjacent to the West Side Highway. The plant was demolished to make way for new construction in 2011. Now under a third generation of management by the Starr family, Artkraft Strauss remains in business by providing design and consulting services.

## CLAUDE NEON LIGHTS INC.

This firm formed on April 1, 1924, as the American subsidiary of Georges Claude's French-based neon sign enterprise. Claude created the world's first commercially practical neon advertising signs in Paris before World War I, and he received various U.S. patents for elements of his "system of neon illumination" in 1915. In the 1920s, Claude attempted to retain sole control of the neon sign business throughout Europe and the United States by selling franchise agreements and litigating against nonlicensed neon sign shops for patent infringement. For most of its tenure, the company

maintained its headquarters at 50 East 42nd Street; its plant was located at 30–20 Thomson Avenue in Long Island City, Queens. Claude Neon Lights produced some of the most prominent neon displays in New York in the 1920s and 1930s. After the expiration of Claude's critical patents in 1932, his company lost ground to smaller shops that quickly came to dominate the neon sign industry in New York. The Serota Sign Corporation purchased Claude Neon Lights Inc. in 1941. Under Serota's ownership, the company survived in name only as Claude Neon Products Inc. through the 1970s. Ownership of Serota ultimately passed to Spectrum Signs Inc. of Farmingdale, Long Island.

## E. G. CLARKE INC.

Little is known of E. G. Clarke Inc., though the firm ranked among New York's most successful electric sign shops for much of the twentieth century. The company participated in New York Edison's first electric sign show, held in 1921. E. G. Clarke produced quantity items, such as neon skeleton signs for Schaefer beer, as well as Times Square spectaculars (in collaboration with Douglas Leigh) for products such as Eveready batteries and Sylvania household appliances. The firm remained active through the early 1960s. At least two of its on-premise displays remain in service some fifty years after their creation.

## GLOBE NEON SIGN CO.

This firm operated variously as the Globe Sign Co., Globe Neon Tube Corp., Globe Neon Signs, the Globe Neon Sign Co., Globe Signs, and finally as the Globe Sign Corp., at a succession of addresses, first in Manhattan and later in the Mott Haven and Hunts Point sections of the Bronx from its origins in 1924 through the 1970s. For much of its life, Globe operated under the direction of David Cheifetz, a colorful character whose sometimes questionable business practices became legendary within the industry. Globe specialized in typical on-premise storefront signs. The company's commissions included the fascia sign for the famous Carnegie Delicatessen on Seventh Avenue in Manhattan (c. 1960), which remains in service more than five decades after its installation. Cheifetz sold

the firm to the Award Sign Co. in the early 1970s, which was subsequently absorbed by the West Side Neon Sign Co.

## HIGGER SIGN CO.

Herman Higger, a Ukrainian immigrant who had trained as an artist in Paris, had difficulty earning a living as an artist after arriving in New York, so he set up shop in 1915 as a sign painter. He was later joined in the business by his younger brother Murray, who remained with the firm until leaving to set up his own shop after World War II. The Higger brothers ventured into the neon business by the 1930s, eventually opening a large shop on Atlantic Avenue in the Bedford-Stuyvesant section of Brooklyn. The firm remained prominent in the industry through the 1950s, but it declined in the following decade after Herman Higger's death. Known in its last years as the Higger Electric Sign Co., the company was finally sold to the Serota Sign Corp. in the late 1960s.

## LA SALLE SIGN CORP.

La Salle was established in 1900 by Joseph Langsner, an artist and sign painter of Polish and Transylvanian descent who had come to the United States at the end of the nineteenth century. The firm operated variously as Joseph Langsner Co. and as the Langsner Sign Co. on the Lower East Side of Manhattan through the mid-1930s. After Joseph Langsner's death around c. 1919, ownership passed to his son, Samuel, who formed a partnership with another immigrant sign painter called Nathan Salzman. They moved the shop to the Clinton Hill section of Brooklyn, where it operated as the La Salle Sign Corp. after 1935. Salzman soon left to form his own firm, and Langsner took full control of the business thereafter. Ownership passed to Samuel's son, Justin Langsner, around 1975. The firm continued to produce and maintain electric signs until Langsner went into semiretirement in 1996.

## MIDTOWN NEON SIGN CORP.

Founded after World War II by brothers Herman (Hy) and Fred (Freddie) Miller. Herman Miller had been in the sign business previously

with another firm; the brothers set up shop on their own after Fred Miller's discharge from military service. Midtown Neon operated from various locations on the west side of Manhattan, with its shop situated for many years at 72 East 110th Street. It specialized in on-premise storefront signs for restaurants and other small businesses, numerous examples of which are still in service more than fifty years after their installation. Notable commissions included the Mutual of New York "Weatherstar" beacon in Syracuse, New York (1965–1966). The company also produced neon tubes for artists, including Robert Rauschenberg and Ron Ferry. At its peak, the firm's payroll included some thirty employees, but business declined after the 1990s and the company ultimately ceased operations in February 2009. A successor firm called Midtown Sign Services has since opened, and it is run by descendants of the Miller brothers.

## RAINBOW LIGHT INC.

Rainbow Light was formed c. 1924 by Raymond R. Machlett, a Cornell-trained physicist whose family's company, E. Machlett & Son, had earned its reputation in the development of X-ray tubes at the turn of the century. Rainbow Light Inc. and its sister firm, Rainbow Luminous Products, emerged as Claude Neon's chief competitors during the 1920s. Machlett claimed to have made and sold some 450 neon signs before Claude organized his American company in April 1924. Like Claude, Rainbow issued franchise agreements to other sign firms, which gave the company a foothold in Los Angeles and Chicago by 1926. Rainbow managed to secure some of New York's most significant neon sign commissions of the 1920s and early 1930s: it supplied tubes for the neon conversion of the enormous roof sign of the Sunshine Biscuits bakery in Long Island City in 1926, for the new marquee and vertical signs of New York's Roxy Theatre on West 50th Street in 1927, and for the marquees and vertical signs of Radio City Music Hall and the RKO Roxy Theatre at Rockefeller Center in 1932. Neither Claude nor Rainbow managed to compete with the smaller sign shops that took over the market in the

1930s; both firms vanished by the end of World War II.

## SALZMAN SIGN CO.

One of the longest-running and most prolific fabricators of on-premise signs for small businesses in the New York area, the Salzman Sign Co. was active from the 1930s through the 1970s. Its owner, a Russian-speaking sign painter named Nathan Salzman, had arrived in the United States in 1914 and had established his own shop by 1930. In the mid-1930s, Salzman partnered with Samuel Langsner to form the La Salle Sign Corp., but he soon went back into business on his own, forming the Salzman Sign Co. at 1001 Bedford Avenue in the Clinton Hill section of Brooklyn. In 1940 Salzman advertised that his services came with the wisdom of "over 25 years in the sign business." The firm's commissions included the vast neon fascia on Nathan's Famous on Surf Avenue at Coney Island (c. 1960), one of numerous examples of its work still in service.

## SEROTA SIGN CORP.

This firm was established before 1930 by Max Serota, a Jewish sign painter who immigrated to the United States from Russia in 1902. Upon Serota's death in 1941, control passed to his son, Theodore (Teddy) Serota, who ran the company for decades. In November 1941, Serota acquired control of Claude Neon Lights Inc., which had formed in 1924 as Georges Claude's first formal venture into the American market. Serota consolidated the activities of both firms at Claude's Long Island City plant, but America's entry into World War II soon forced the company to suspend normal operations, thus derailing whatever plans Serota may have had for the merger. After the war, Serota moved the company's plant to the Bronx, where it prospered as one of New York's most prominent makers of on-premise displays. Ownership eventually passed to Welsbach Electric, an electrical contractor, which later sold the company to Spectrum Signs Inc. of Farmingdale, Long Island.

## SILVERESCENT NEON SIGN CO.

Silverescent was formed by the brothers Silvio and Salvatore (Sally) Sanzo around 1932. After World War II the Sanzo brothers sold the firm to Murray Higger, formerly of the Higger Sign Co. (The Sanzo brothers remained with the firm for many years.) Higger resuscitated the company from a nearly defunct state and gradually built it into one of the most successful fabricators of on-premise electric signs in the New York area, eventually employing as many as twenty-five people at its shop in Bushwick, Brooklyn. Many of its signs bore the stylistic influence of Charlie Klein, the company's veteran layout man. Upon Murray Higger's retirement in the mid-1970s, ownership passed to his son, Alfred, who ran the business until his own retirement in 1996. At that point, the firm ceased its sign production activities and sold its maintenance contracts to a consortium that eventually became part of Spectrum Signs of Farmingdale, Long Island. A successor firm called United Sign Systems of Oldsmar, Florida, carries on in the tradition its predecessor under the ownership of one of Higger's descendants.

## SUPER NEON LIGHTS INC.

Established c. 1942 by James Coccaro, an artist and sign painter, in Bensonhurst, Brooklyn, Super Neon Lights rose to prominence over the years as a maker of on-premise neon signs for storefronts, especially in predominantly Italian-American Brooklyn neighborhoods such as Bensonhurst, Bay Ridge, Dyker Heights, and Gravesend. Its commissions have included the original storefront sign for Sbarro's, which opened as a small grosseria in Bensonhurst in the mid-1950s and later grew to become an internationally franchised chain pizzeria. Super Neon Lights continues to fabricate, install, and service neon signs under a second generation of management by the Coccaro family.

## UNIVERSAL ELECTRIC SIGN CO.

This firm was formed after World War II by Manny Schneider, an attorney and adept businessman who managed to secure contracts to provide neon skeleton signs for various beer producers while the neon industry was dormant during the war. The company set up shop in Ridgewood, near the border of Brooklyn and Queens. It later operated as the Universal Point of Sales Corp., and later still as Universal Unlimited, eventually relocating to Glen Cove, Long Island. Specializing in neon skeleton signs produced in quantity, the company grew to become one of the largest neon shops in the New York area, employing as many as forty glass benders at its peak. The firm later diversified its services into other types of signs, winning the contract to fabricate and install the enormous "Met Life" display atop the former Pan Am building on Park Avenue in Manhattan in 1992–1993, before ceasing operations shortly thereafter.

## WEST SIDE NEON SIGN CO.

The firm was established in the years immediately following World War II by Gus Schlesinger, an Austrian immigrant, and headquartered at 972 Amsterdam Avenue in Manhattan. In about 1956, Gus went into partnership with Max Leschowitz and Michael Lettera. Leschowitz was a veteran sheet metal man who had emigrated from Eastern Europe to Manhattan. Lettera, the son of Italian immigrants, began his career at thirteen as an apprentice tube bender for a firm called City Wide Neon Signs in East Harlem. Considerably younger than his partners, Lettera bought out their shares in the business when Schlesinger and Leschowitz eventually retired. West Side Neon prospered in the 1960s and 1970s with contracts to assemble and service scoreboards at Madison Square Garden and Yankee Stadium, employing a staff of about fifty persons at its peak. The firm moved to the Bronx by 1965, eventually opening a large plant on Bronx River Avenue. Lettera sold the company to the Artkraft Strauss Sign Corp. in 1988, and he retired from the business five years later. His sons later opened a successor firm, the Lettera Sign & Electric Co., which operates as one of New York's most prominent sign shops today.

# NOTES

p. 13: **In his 1850 travelogue**—Foster, *New York by Gas-Light*, 71, 113.

**Internally lit "shadow-box"**—Jakle, *City Lights*, 27.

p. 14: **Gaslit signs advertised hotels, restaurants, and especially theaters, such as Tony Pastor's New York music halls."**—Caldwell, *New York Night*, 126.

E. A. Mills, the manager of the Electric Sign Bureau of the New York Edison Co., provided this description of gaslit signs: "As a rule they were of box construction, with the gas jets inside. The sides of the box were usually studded with vari-colored glass jewels outlining the letters. These signs were usually found outside of drug stores, oyster houses, etc. There was another type of gas illuminated sign which could be used only indoors, as it was readily extinguished by every slight breeze. This sign was made up of copper tubing bent in the shape of letters, and drilled at regular intervals, and the gas pressure so regulated that only a tiny flame was emitted. The result was very striking, even though the sign was more or less of a fire risk." —*Signs of the Times*, May 1922.

**. . . the first electric sign**—O. P. Anderson, "Brief Outline of Electric Sign History and Development," *Signs of the Times*, May 1922.

**The world's first large electrified commercial billboard**—Nye, *Electrifying America*, 50.

**The 'Ocean Breezes' sign disappeared**—Starr and Hayman, *Signs and Wonders*, 57.

**. . . references to Broadway as the "Great white way"**—Bloom, *Broadway*, 499.

For more on O. J. Gude, see "The Napoleon of Publicity," in Tell, *Times Square Spectacular*, 52. A nationwide concern called the General Outdoor Advertising Company (GOAC) absorbed O. J. Gude in 1925. The GOAC survived until being taken over by advertising conglomerate Metromedia in 1964.

p. 15: **Miner's Fifth Avenue Theatre**—E. A. Mills, "The Development of Electric Sign Lighting," *Signs of the Times*, May 1922.

**a rate of about two hundred every month."**—Arthur Williams, "Broadway—A Fascinating Electric Sign Picture Gallery," *Signs of the Times*, May 1917.

**To reduce glare and improve legibility**—Mills, "Development of Electric Sign Lighting."

p. 16: **New York Edison went into high gear**—"Representative Exhibits at New York Edison Electric Sign Show, May 2 to 11," *Signs of the Times*, June 1921.

**"What makes New York's Great White Way light"**—"9,577 Electric Signs Using 1,000,000 Lamps Disclosed by New York City's Sign Survey," *Signs of the Times*, March 1923.

**The 1923 survey tallied 9,577 electric signs**—"Why the Great White Way Is So White," *Signs of the Times*, May 1925.

**The total rose to 18,958**—"New York Sign Show Success," *Signs of the Times*, April 1927.

**Another survey**—"Why Your Electric Display Should be Claude Neon Tube Signs" (advertisement), *New York Times*, October 18, 1927.

**Experiments based on this technology**—Mel Morris traces the origins of the neon luminous tube to experiments conducted by Jean Picard in 1676; Rudi Stern cites experiments by Otto von Guericke of Magdeburg in 1683. See Morris, *Neon Tube Sign Business*, 3, and Stern, *New Let There Be Neon*, 16.

**. . . the short life of the tube"**—Morris describes a shadow-box sign using Geissler tubes in Morris, "History of the Neon Luminous Tube Trade Had Beginning with Electricity," *Signs of the Times*, December 1927.

p. 17: **"The incandescent electric lamp of to-day"**—Moore, "The Light of the Future," *Cassier's Magazine*, July 1894.

**Neon gas had yet to be discovered**—Morris, *History of the Neon Luminous Tube*, p. 45.

**"The coming cylinders of light will glow"**—Moore, "The Light of the Future," *Cassier's Magazine*, July 1894.

**"It is hardly too much to say"**—"Light Will Float Like Perfume," *Los Angeles Times*, July 22, 1894.

**Moore tubes began to appear**—"Advances in Vacuum Tube Lighting," *Chicago Daily Tribune*, June 2, 1896.

**"Two years later he mocked up a small, tube-lit chapel . . . for the Electrical Exhibition of 1898."**—"The Moore Exhibit at Madison Square," *The Electrical Engineer*, May 12, 1898.

**Permanent Moore tube installations appeared**—"Artificial Daylight Floods Garden's Lobby," *New York Times*, December 22, 1905.

p. 18: **"It was not like any sign"**—"Daylight Seen in Tubes," *New York Times*, May 8, 1897.

**"Soon the long-tube installations became commonplace"**—Morris, *Rare Gas Neon White Light*, 4–5.

**The trouble with the Moore"**—Morris, "History of the Neon Luminous Tube," 45. See also Jakle, 79.

**According to one account**—Morris, *Neon Tube Sign Business*, 5.

**Claude obtained Moore's permission**—Morris, *Neon Patent Situation*, 5.

p. 19: **"The blaze of crimson light"**—Travers, *Discovery of the Rare Gases*, 95–97.

**Moore reportedly had difficulty**—Morris, *Neon Patent Situation*, 5.

**One account credits the first neon advertising**—Morris, "First Commercial Neon Sign Built by Madine and Trimble in 1909," *Signs of the Times*, October 1928.

p. 20: **"As is known the color of the light emitted by neon"**—Morris, *Neon Patent Situation*, 61.

**Historians provide differing accounts**—Various secondary sources describe Claude's first neon sign as having been made for a Paris coiffeur sometime between 1911 and 1913. See Starr and Hayman and Stern, 23.

**Claude came to the United**—Morris, *Neon Patent Situation*, 5.

**Indicative of the early reception**—Stern, 23.

**He made no further significant effort**—Madine and Trimble's earlier sign notwithstanding, various secondary sources have cited signs installed at Earl Anthony's Los Angeles and San Francisco Packard dealerships as the first commercial neon installations to appear in the United States

since at least as early as a September 1927 article published in *Signs of the Times*. See F. A. Orth, "Neon is Greatest Penetrator of All Lights," *Signs of the Times*, September 1927.

**Early customers included chain stores**—"Luminous Gas Lights New Electric Sign," *Signs of the Times*, October 1924, and "John Ward Men's Shoes," *The Edison Monthly*, November 1924. Primary sources identifying New York's first true neon sign are elusive; Tama Starr and Edward Hayman identify New York's first neon spectacular as one built for Willys-Overland Motors at Broadway and West 45th Street by Claude in association with the Strauss Sign Company in 1924. Starr and Hayman, 86.

**Claude Neon's American profits**—Morris, *Neon Patent Situation*, 3.

**But with the expiration of his American patents**—Miller and Fink, *Neon Signs*, 6.

p. 21: **Neon consumed much less electricity**—Retrofitting incandescent signs with neon tubes was a relatively common practice; see H. S. Parker, "Rebuilt Displays: An Economical Way to Sign Modernization," *Signs of the Times*, July 1932, 29. Prominent examples in New York included the roof sign at Tudor City, retrofitted in 1939.

p. 23: **. . . Local 230 of the Sign Pictorial**—Interviews with Gasper Ingui, Alfred Higger, and Justin Langsner, October 2010–February 2011. For more on the sign painters' school, see Abraham Switkin, "New York's Newest Sign School," *Signs of the Times*, June 1946.

p. 25: **Signs of the Times featured New York storefront signs**—See "Vahan Hagopian," *Signs of the Times*, November 1932; Horace Ginsbern, "In Store-Front Displays . . . Harmonious Design Is Still the modern Advertising Force," *Signs of the Times*, June 1934; Morris Lapidus, "Where the Sign Begins . . . ," *Signs of the Times*, September 1934.

**New York's most significant surviving architect-designed neon**—"Nine Display Units Constitute Radio City Music Hall's Electrical Advertising," *Signs of the Times*, March 1933.

p. 26: **At least three schools of neon glass**—Advertisements for the Egani Technical Institute, *Signs of the Times*, October 1948, and the Neon School of New York, *Signs of the Times*, March 1949.

p. 27 **Colored glass tubes**—The history and process of Corning's neon tube production is described in Julian Kilman, "Glass Eyes for the Sign," *Signs of the Times*, January 1948.

p. 28 **Finally, the introduction of tubes lined with fluorescent**—William W. Anthony Jr., "A Brief History of the Sign Industry," *Signs of the Times*, September 1976.

**New York sign shops typically expected**—Interviews with Gasper Ingui, November 6, 2010, and Justin Langsner, February 21, 2011.

p. 30 **Though it was used for electric signs . . . porcelain enamel**—Interviews with Gasper Ingui, Alfred Higger, and Justin Langsner, October 2010–February 2011, and "Sub-Contracted Sign Services," *Signs of the Times*, June 1936.

**"Try to think of two sign materials"**—Advertisement for ARMCO, *Signs of the Times*, February 1945.

**Sign makers began using aluminum**—"Aluminum Signs," advertisement for Aluminum Sign Co., *Signs of the Times*, July 1912.

p. 33 **At their best, electric signs could**—Burr L. Robins, president of the General Outdoor Advertising Co., quoted in Blake, 11.

**"commercially-financed light sculpture"**—Starr and Hayman, 5.

**In seventeenth-century Paris**—Schivelbusch, *Disenchanted Night*, 84–85.

**Such abuses spurred an organized movement"**—Starr and Hayman, *Signs and Wonders*, 27. See also John DeWitt Warner, "Advertising Run Mad," *Municipal Affairs*, June 1900.

**Under the headline "Advertising Run Mad,"**—Warner, "Advertising Run Mad," *Municipal Affairs*, June 1900.

**In 1910, the Municipal Art Society**—"Ugly Electric Signs Mar Fifth Avenue." *New York Times*, July 8, 1910.

**"Electric signs have become so numerous"**—"Ugly Electric Signs Mar Fifth Avenue." *New York Times*, July 8, 1910.

**Antisign interests persuaded City Hall**—"Sky Sign Converts Turn on Forty-Second Street," *New York Times*, March 31, 1922.

the *New York Times* **reported**—"Sky Sign Converts Turn on Forty-Second Street," *New York Times*, March 31, 1922.

**"threatened eclipse of the midnight sun"**—"All Attempts to Dim Times Square Signs Opposed by Business Men," *Signs of the Times*, June 1922. See also Nye, *American Technological Sublime*, 173–98.

**"By the 1920s photographers and painters"**—Nye, *Electrifying America*, 29; Nye, *American Technological Sublime*, 173.

**"Fire signs announcing the night's"**—Dreiser, *Sister Carrie*, 308.

**Later, Dreiser called the "Ocean Breezes" sign**—Dreiser, *Color of a Great City*, 119.

**Similar romantic characterizations**—This is charted in great detail in Sharpe, *New York Nocturne*, and in Nye, *Electrifying America*.

**"bejewled with all manner of electrical"**—Martin, "Manhattan Lights," *Harper's Monthly Magazine*, February 1906.

p. 34 **That same year more than 40,000 feet of neon tubing**—"Sign Art at the World's Fair," *Signs of the Times*, July 1933.

p. 35 **"In a walk-up room, filled with the intermittent flashing"**—Higham and Greenberg, *Hollywood in the Forties*, 19. The film historians Alain Silver and James Ursini identify this as the first usage of the term "film noir" in the English language: see Silver and Ursini, *Film Noir Reader*, 12.

**"With the repeal of prohibition"**—Miller and Fink, *Neon Signs*, 6.

p. 36 **"life in the raw"**—Algren, *Neon Wilderness*, back cover copy, 1949 edition.

**"This was the jungle, the neon wilderness"**—Algren, *Neon Wilderness*, 165.

**"Right across the street there was trouble"**—Kerouac, *On the Road*, 85.

**"Along that strip"**—Rechy, *City of Night*, 148.

p. 37 **The precipitous decline of Times**—Historians have traced the decline of Times Square to the proliferation of burlesque houses on 42nd Street during the Great Depression as business-starved theaters lowered standards to draw crowds. See Tell,

*Times Square Spectacular*, and Sagalyn, *Times Square Roulette*.

**"Giant signs-Bigger! Than! Life!"**—Rechy, *City of Night*, 30.

p. 38 **"This means turning away from luminous-tubing displays"**—"Goodyear's 'Newest Thing,'" *Signs of the Times*, March 1938.

p. 39 **With the introduction of fluorescent lamps . . . use of fluorescent lamps in outdoor advertising."**—See "Transmitted Light Signs," *The Magazine of Light*, 1938.

**New York sign shops began installing fluorescent lamp signs**—Alfred Higger recalls General Electric field representatives assisting his family's sign shop, the Higger Sign Co., in the installation of a fluorescent sign for an outlet of the Sodamat chain on the Coney Island boardwalk around the time of the 1939 New York World's Fair. Interview with Alfred Higger, December 16, 2010.

**Acrylic resin plastic, Rohm & Haas advised**—D. S. Frederick, "Acrylic Resin Plastics . . . for Sign Uses," *Signs of the Times*, October 1939.

**"The designers of the New York fair'"**—F. W. Fuller and J. A. McDermott, "Luminous Tube Lighting at the New York World's Fair," *Signs of the Times*, September 1939.

p. 40 **In** *God's Own Junkyard*—Blake, 33.

**"The S.O.S. program resulted in the removal of a large number of obsolete and unsightly signs"**—NESA advertisement, *Signs of the Times*, May 1966, 118.

**"Neon is the purest, hippest color"**—"A Times Square State of Mind." *Time*, March 18, 1966.

**"Neon in daylight is a great pleasure"**—O'Hara, *Lunch Poems*.

p. 41 **Artists such as the Czech sculptor Dietmar**—"Licht als Metapher—Kunst mit Neon," in Weibel and Janson, *Light Art from Artificial Light*.

**"Architects . . . do not easily acknowledge the validity of the commercial vernacular."**—Venturi, Brown and Izenour, *Learning from Las Vegas*, 6.

**"the deadness that results from too great a preoccupation with tastefulness**

**and total design"**—Venturi, Brown and Izenour, 53.

**"'Save those old neon signs!' advised** *Signs of the Times* **in a 1974 story: 'There's more value in many of them than the junk dealer will offer.'"**—"Let There Be Neon," *Signs of the Times*, December 1974.

**". . . an 'interminable wasteland"**—Blake, 8.

p. 42 **A 2011 survey by** *Signs of the Times*—Wade Swormstedt, "The 2011 Electric State of the Industry Report," *Signs of the Times*, July 2011.

p. 43 **"The warehouse district of Lower Manhattan . . . serves fine nouvelle cuisine"**—Moira Hodgson, "French Nouvelle and Classic Cuisine," *New York Times*, November 14, 1980.

**"One of the tallest, most prominently situated skyscrapers"**—Blake, 127.

**"Couldn't they just leave the sign"**—Arthur Higbee, "American Topics," *New York Times*, September 9, 1992.

p. 44 **"Once Pan Am had gone out of business"**—Paul Goldberger, "Signs of Lost Times," *New York Times*, May 14, 1994.

**"Signs in Times Square are like redwoods"**—James Brooke, "Conserving the Glitter of Times Square." *New York Times*, May 11, 1986. A thorough description of the movement to save the Times Square signs is provided in Starr and Hayman, 236–55.

**The commission unanimously rejected the proposed removal**—Christopher Gray, "Streetscapes: Tudor City; Landmarks Won't Let a Co-op Fiddle with Its Roof," *New York Times*, November 26, 1995.

p. 45 **"one of the sharpest visual intrusions the midtown skyline has seen in years"**—Paul Goldberger, "Critic's Notebook," *New York Times*, January 9, 1986.

**"We wish we could shoot the stupid thing down altogether"**—Clyde Haberman, "Drying Out the Red Neon Umbrella," *New York Times*, May 19, 1998.

**The historic village of Rhinebeck**—John Davis, "Realtor, Rhinebeck Feud over TV as Sign in Store Window." *Poughkeepsie Journal*, February 14, 2011.

**Officials in Chatham Borough, New Jersey"**—David W. Chen, "Graceful or Gaudy? As Towns Ban Signs, Merchants Fight Back." *New York Times*, March 14, 1995.

**"obnoxious, offensive and out of context"**—Kevin Zawaci, "Debate over Sign May Prevent Walgreen's from Opening in Nyack," *Nyack Piermont Patch* (online), September 16, 2010.

**. . . preservationists in New Orleans rallied to protect . . . the same stretch of Canal Street**—Keli Rylance, "Help Protect Landmark Neon Signage," DOCOMOMO US/Louisiana, August 6, 2010.

p. 46: **A November 2010 survey**—"Which Times Square Do You Prefer," gothamist.com, November 8, 2010.

**A blog entitled "Lost City"**—"Lost City," http://lostnewyorkcity.blogspot.com/, retrieved December 17, 2008.

**"Astoundingly, almost one-third of the stores pictured here have disappeared."**—Murray and Murray, *Storefront*, 6.

p. 47: **"Dick's old place was dirty and it smelled like the zoo"**—Mitchell, *Up in the Old Hotel*, 244–45.

**"They are of a day prior to the advent of skyscrapersw"**—Charles G. Shaw, "Ancient Trade Signs in Modern New York," *The Magazine Antiques*, October 1938.

**"A man born in New York forty years ago"**—*Harper's New Monthly Magazine*, June-November 1856, quoted in Fogelson, *Downtown*.

**"how swiftly and steadily the city was changing**—Dreiser, *Color of a Great City*, vvi

**The pace of change in the postwar years**—For more, see Anthony Wood, *Preserving New York: Winning the Right to Protect a City's Landmarks* (New York: Routledge, 2007), and Randall Mason, *The Once and Future New York* (Minneapolis: University of Minnesota Press, 2009).

p. 48: **"Our city is molting"**—Justin Davidson, "The Glass Stampede," *New York Magazine*, September 7, 2008.

# MONTAGE CAPTIONS

**page 5**

(first row): Air Line Diner, 69-35 Astoria Boulevard, Queens, c. 1952; Smith's Bar and Restaurant, 701 Eighth Avenue, Manhattan, 1954; Patsy's Restaurant, 236 West 56th Street, Manhattan, 1954; Russ & Daughters Appetizers, 179 E. Houston Street, Manhattan, 1951

(second row): Subway Inn, 14 East 60th Street, Manhattan, c. 1955; Hinsch's Confectionary, 8518 Fifth Avenue, Brooklyn, c. 1948; Carnegie Delicatessen, 854 Seventh Avenue, Manhattan, c. 1960; Clover Delicatessen, 621 Second Avenue, Manhattan, 1956

(third row): Maiman's Pharmacy, 821 Franklin Avenue, Brooklyn, c. 1951; Nathan's Famous, Inc., 1310 Surf Avenue, Brooklyn, c. 1960; Estates Pharmacy, 169-01 Hillside Avenue, Queens, c. 1940

(fourth row): Carnegie Delicatessen, 854 Seventh Avenue, Manhattan, c. 1960; Joe Abbracciamento Restaurant, 62-96 Woodhaven Boulevard, Queens, c. 1949; Pepsi-Cola, Long Island City, Queens, 1936; Block Drugs, 101 Second Avenue, Manhattan, 1945

**page 8**

(from top): Waverly Theater, 323 Fifth Avenue, Manhattan, c. 1985; D'Aiuto Pastry Corp., 405 Eighth Avenue, Manhattan, 1960; Katz's Delicatessen, 205 E. Houston Street, Manhattan, 1935; Tom's Restaurant, 2880 Broadway, Manhattan, 1957; Cheyenne Diner, 411 Ninth Avenue, Manhattan, c. 1980; Clover Delicatessen, 621 Second Avenue, Manhattan, 1956

**page 10**

(top right): New Covenant Holiness Church, 512 West 157th Street, Manhattan, c. 1980; (top left): Iglesia De Dios Pentecostal, 563 W 187th St, Manhattan, c. 1990; (bottom left): Temple Healing From Heaven, 2535 Frederick Douglass Boulevard, Manhattan; (bottom right): The Father's Heart Ministries, 545 East 11th Street, Manhattan, c. 1965; (Center): St. Paul's House, 335 West 51st Street, Manhattan, c. 1950 (facsimile, c. 2007)

**page 31**

(first row): Estates Pharamacy, 169-01 Hillside Avenue, Queens, c. 1940; Capitol Fishing Tackle Co., 132 West 36th Street, Manhattan, 1941; Catania's Shoe Shop, 3015 Westchester Avenue, Bronx, c. 1945; Morscher's Pork Store, 5844 Catalpa Avenue, Queens, c. 1950

(second row): Ridgewood Carpet, 6001 Myrtle Avenue, Queens, c. 1951; White Horse Tavern, 567 Hudson Street, Manhattan, 1946; Neergaard Drugs, 454 Fifth Avenue, Manhattan, c. 1950; Farrell's Bar & Grill, 215 Prospect Park West, Brooklyn, c. 1935

(third row): Reynold's Bar, 710 W180th Street, Manhattan, c. 1959; Louis Zuflacht Furniture, 154 Stanton Street, Manhattan, 1942; Vasikauskas Bar & Grill, 279 Grand Street, Brooklyn, c. 1950; Famous Oyster Bar, 842 Seventh Avenue, Manhattan, c. 1960

(fourth row): Frank's Sporting Goods, 430 East Tremont Avenue, Bronx, 1949; Clover Delicatessen, 621 Second Avenue, Manhattan, 1956; Deno's Wonder Wheel Amusement Park, 3059 West 12th Street, Brooklyn, c. 1950; Crown Caterers, 4909 13th Avenue, Brooklyn, c. 1949

**page 38**

(top row): Gun Hill Fence, 4171 Boston Road, Bronx, c. 1959; Nagengast Hardware, 6802 Fresh Pond Road, Queens, c. 1956; Rubinstein and Klein Furniture, 6001 14th Avenue, Brooklyn, c. 1965; Toy Store, 909 Kings Highway, Brooklyn, c. 1955

(bottom row): Meat Palace, 1854 Nostrand Avenue, Brooklyn, c. 1950; Allied Travel, 1455 Bedford Avenue, Brooklyn, c. 1955; Stratford Fuel, 1162 East Tremont Avenue, Bronx, c. 1952; Columbus Hardware, 852 Ninth Avenue, Manhattan, c. 1955

# SELECTED BIBLIOGRAPHY

## BOOKS

Agnew, Hugh E. *Outdoor Advertising.* New York: McGraw-Hill, 1938.

Algren, Nelson. *The Neon Wilderness.* New York: Avon, 1949.

Atkinson, Frank H. *Sign Painting Up to Now.* Chicago: Frederick J. Drake, c. 1915.

Auer, Michael J. *Preservation Brief No. 25: The Preservation of Historic Signs.* Washington, D.C.: National Park Service, 1991.

Becker, Alf R. *100 Alphabets.* Cincinnati: Signs of the Times Publishing, 1941.

Berman, Marshall, and Brian Berger, eds. *New York Calling: From Blackout to Bloomberg.* London: Reaktion, 2007.

Biegeleisen, John I. *The Book of 100 Type Face Alphabets: A Guide to Better Lettering.* Cincinnati: Signs of the Times Publishing, 1965.

Blake, Peter. *God's Own Junkyard: The Planned Deterioration of the American Landscape.* New York: Holt, Rinehart, and Winston, 1964.

Bloom, Ken. *Broadway: Its History, People, and Places: An Encyclopedia.* New York: Routledge, 2003.

Caldwell, Marc. *New York Night: The Mystique and Its History.* New York: Scribner, 2005.

Cromwell, J. Howard. *A System of Easy Lettering.* New York: Spon & Chamberlain, 1900.

*Cyclopedia of Applied Electricity. Chicago: American Technical Society,* 1919.

Davidson, Len. *Vintage Neon.* Atglen, Pa.: Schiffer, 1999.

DiLemme, Philip. *Luminous Advertising Sketches: A Treatise on Electric Signs, Store Front Designs, Abstracts on Modern Alphabets.* New York: White House Publications, 1953.

Dreiser, Theodore. *The Color of a Great City.* New York: Howard Fertig, 1987.

———. *Sister Carrie.* New York: Literary Classics of the United States, 1987.

*Essentials of Outdoor Advertising.* New York: Association of National Advertisers, 1958.

Evans, Bill, and Andrew Larson. *Shopfronts.* New York: Van Nostrand Reinhold, 1981.

Fogelson, Robert M. *Downtown: Its Rise and Fall, 1880–1950.* New Haven: Yale University Press, 2001.

Foster, George G. *New York by Gas-Light.* Berkeley: University of California Press, 1990. Reprint of 1850 edition, published by DeWitt & Davenport, New York.

Freeland, David. *Automats, Taxi Dances, and Vaudeville: Excavating Manhattan's Lost Places of Leisure.* New York: New York University Press, 2009.

Frizot, Michel, ed. *New History of Photography.* Köln: Könemann, 1998.

Gordon, William Hugh. *Lettering for Commercial Purposes.* Cincinnati: Signs of the Times Publishing, 1926.

Hammett, Jerilou, and Kingsley Hammer, eds. *The Suburbanization of New York.* New York: Princeton Architectural Press, 2007.

Heimann, Jim, and Rib Georges. *California Crazy: Roadside Vernacular Architecture.* San Francisco: Chronicle, 1980.

Higham, Charles, and Joel Greenberg. *Hollywood in the Forties.* London: A. Zwemmer, 1968.

Houck, John W, ed. *Outdoor Advertising History and Regulation.* Notre Dame: University of Notre Dame Press, 1969.

*Illuminating Engineering Practice.* New York: McGraw-Hill, 1917.

Jackson, John Brinckerhoff. *Landscape in Sight: Looking at America.* New Haven: Yale University Press, 1997.

Jacobs, Jane. *The Death and Life of Great American Cities.* New York: Random House, 2002.

Jakle, John A. *City Lights: Illuminating the American Night.* Baltimore: Johns Hopkins University Press, 2001.

Jester, Thomas C., ed. *Twentieth-Century Building Materials: History and Conservation.* New York: McGraw-Hill, 1995.

Kerouac, Jack. *On the Road.* New York: Penguin, 1976.

Klein, Jef. *The History and Stories of the Best Bars of New York.* Nashville, Tenn.: Turner Publishing, 2006.

Klein, William. *Life Is Good and Good for You in New York.* Manchester, U.K.: Dewi Lewis, 1995.

Koolhaas, Rem. *Delirious New York: A Retroactive Manifesto for Manhattan.* New York: Monacelli Press, 1994.

Liebs, Chester H. *Main Street to Miracle Mile: American Roadside Architecture.* Boston: Little, Brown, 1985.

Lippincott, Wilmot. *Outdoor Advertising.* New York: McGraw-Hill, 1923.

Lowenthal, David. *The Past Is a Foreign Country.* Cambridge: Cambridge University Press, 1985.

Margolies, John. *End of the Road.* New York: Penguin, 1981.

Mendelsohn, Erich. *Amerika: Bilderbuch eines Architekten.* Braunschweig: Fredr. Vieweg & Sohn Verlagsgesellschaft, 1991.

Miller, Samuel C., and Donald G. Fink. *Neon Signs: Manufacture—Installation—Maintenance.* New York: McGraw-Hill, 1935.

Miller, William. *Outdoor Advertising Design.* New York: General Outdoor Advertising, 1958.

Mitchell, Joseph. *Up in the Old Hotel.* New York: Vintage, 2008.

Morris, Mel. *The Neon Patent Situation.* Houston: Mel Morris Neon Laboratories, 1930.

———. *The Neon Tube Sign Business.* Houston: Mel Morris Neon Laboratories, 1929.

———. *The Rare Gas Neon White Light.* Houston: Mel Morris Neon Laboratories, 1929.

Murray, James, and Karla Murray. *Storefront: The Disappearing Face of Old New York.* Corte Madera, Calif.: Gingko Press, 2008.

Neumann, Dietrich, with Kermit Swiler Champa et al. *Architecture of the Night.* London: Prestel, 2002.

Nye, David E. *American Technological Sublime.* Cambridge, Mass.: MIT Press, 1994.

———. *Electrifying America: Social Meanings of a New Technology.* Cambridge, Mass.: MIT Press, 1990.

O'Hara, Frank. *Lunch Poems.* San Francisco: City Lights Books, 1964.

Rampersad, Arnold. *The Life of Langston Hughes. Vol. 2.* Oxford: Oxford University Press, 1988.

Rechy, John. *City of Night.* New York: Grove, 1963.

Sagalyn, Lynne B. *Times Square Roulette: Remaking the City Icon.* Cambridge, Mass.: MIT Press, 2001.

Sante, Luc. *Low Life.* London: Granta, 1991.

Schivelbusch, Wolfgang. *Disenchanted Night: The Industrialization of Light in the Nineteenth Century.* Berkeley: University of California Press, 1995.

Sharpe, William Chapman. *New York Nocturne: The City after Dark in Literature, Painting and Photography.* Princeton: Princeton University Press, 2008.

Shaw, Charles G. *New York, Oddly Enough.* New York: Farrar & Rinehart, 1938.

Silver, Alan, and James Ursini. *Film Noir Reader.* New York: Limelight, 2004.

Starr, Tama, and Edward Hayman. *Signs and Wonders: The Spectacular Marketing of America.* New York: Currency, 1998.

Stern, Robert A. M., Gregory Gilmartin, and John Massengale. *New York 1900: Metropolitan Architecture and Urbanism, 1890–1915.* New York: Rizzoli, 1983.

Stern, Robert A. M., Gregory Gilmartin, and Thomas Mellins. *New York 1930: Architecture and Urbanism between* the Two World Wars. New York: Rizzoli, 1987.

Stern, Rudi. *The New Let There Be Neon*. New York: Harry N. Abrams, 1988.

Tell, Darcy. *Times Square Spectacular*. New York: HarperCollins, 2007.

Travers, Morris William. *The Discovery of the Rare Gases*. London: Edward Arnold, 1928.

Venturi, Robert, Denise Scott Brown, and Steven Izenour. *Learning from Las Vegas: The Forgotten Symbolism of Architectural Form*. Cambridge, Mass.: MIT Press, 1977.

Wagner, Charles L. H. *The Story of Signs*. Boston: Arthur MacGibbon, 1954.

Weeks, Edward M. *Letters Analyzed and Spaced*. New York: Exposition Press, c. 1953.

Weibel, Peter, and Gregor Janson, eds. *Light Art from Artificial Light: Light as a Medium in the Art of the 20th and 21st Centuries*. Ostfildern, Germany: Hatje Cantz, 2006.

Weigel, Margaret. *"The Commoditable Block Party: Electric Signs in Manhattan, 1881–1917."* Ph.D. diss., Massachusetts Institute of Technology, 2002.

White, Norval, and Elliot Willensky. *AIA Guide to New York City*. New York: Three Rivers Press, 2000.

Zukin, Sharon. *Naked City: The Death and Life of American Urban Places*. Oxford: Oxford University Press, 2010.

### PERIODICALS

*Chain Store Age*

*The Claude Neon News*

*The Edison Monthly*

*The Magazine of Light*

*The Poster*

*The New York Times*, especially:

" 'Artificial Daylight' Floods Garden's Lobby." December 22, 1905.

"Daylight Seen in Tubes." May 8, 1897.

Dunlap, David W. "The X Files." January 21, 2007.

———. "Workers Expose a Memory of a Bygone Times Square." November 22, 2006.

Gray, Christopher. "Streetscapes: Tudor City; Landmarks Won't Let a Co-op Fiddle with Its Roof." November 26, 1995.

Hodgson, Moira. "French Nouvelle and Classic Cuisine." November 14, 1980.

"Neon Nostalgia from Times Square to Be Sold by Sign Maker." May 15, 2006.

"Sky Sign Converts Turn on Forty-Second Street." March 31, 1922.

"Ugly Electric Signs Mar Fifth Avenue." July 8, 1910.

Wadler, Joyce. "The Restaurateur Who Invented Downtown." January 18, 2004.

*Signs of the Times*, especially:

"All Attempts to Dim Times Square Signs Opposed by Business Men." June 1922.

Anderson, O. P. "Brief Outline of Electric Sign History and Development." May 1916.

Anthony, William W., Jr. "A Brief History of the Sign Industry." September 1976, 62–67.

"Luminous Gas Lights New Electric Sign." October 1924, 47.

Mills, E. A. "The Development of Electric Sign Lighting—Some Early History of the Medium." May 1922, 52–56.

and

Warner, John DeWitt. "Advertising Run Mad." *Municipal Affairs*, June 1900.

Zapatka, Christian. "The Edison Effect: The History of Lighting in the American City." *Lotus International* 75 (1993), 60–77.

"Advances in Vacuum Tube Lighting." *Chicago Daily Tribune*, June 2, 1896.

"Cold Light at Last." *The Boston Globe*, August 1, 1897.

"Inventor's Record." *The Electrical Engineer*, Vol. XXII.

"Light Will Float Like Perfume." *Los Angeles Times*, July 22, 1894.

Martin, Edward S. "Manhattan Lights." *Harper's Monthly Magazine*, February 1907.

Moore, D. McFarlan. "The Light of the Future." *Cassier's Magazine*, July 1894.

"The Moore Exhibit at Madison Square." *The Electrical Engineer*, May 12, 1898. *Outdoor Advertising*

Pujol, Rolando. "Q&A with Koch." *amNewYork*, August 10, 2007.

"A Report on the Moore Tube Lamp." *The Electrical Review*, August 18, 1906.

Sante, Luc. "My Lost City." *New York Review of Books*, November 6, 2003.

Schwarz, Benjamin. "Gentrification and Its Discontents." *Atlantic Monthly*, June 2010.

"Signs and Symbols." *Architectural Record*, September 1956.

### INTERVIEWS

Jeff Friedman
Meryl Gaitan
Scott Hershman
Alfred Higger
Steven Higger
Gasper Ingui
Robert Ingui
Max Langhurst
Justin Langsner
Tama Starr

### ARCHIVES CONSULTED

Avery Architectural and Fine Arts Library at Columbia University
Department of Buildings of the City of New York
Municipal Archives of the City of New York
New-York Historical Society

# ILLUSTRATION CREDITS

Photos and illustrations not credited below are by the author.

13 (center) Photo by Myrna Suárez.

14 (left) Mitchell, Vance & Co. Catalog, c. 1876, reproduced in Picture Book of Authentic Mid-Victorian Gas Lighting Fixtures, New York: Dover, 1984; (right) Photos by Percy Loomis Sperr, collection of the New York Public Library.

15 Photo by William Gottlieb, collection of the Library of Congress.

16 (left) Signs of the Times, October 1923, ST Media Group, used with permission; (center top) Signs of the Times, October 1924, ST Media Group, used with permission; (center bottom) Signs of the Times, November 1922, ST Media Group, used with permission; (right) Signs of the Times, March 1927, ST Media Group, used with permission.

17 Signs of the Times, March 1927, 42. ST Media Group, used with permission.

18 Signs of the Times, May 1929, ST Media Group, used with permission.

19 (left) Morris, The Neon Tube Sign Business, Houston: Mel Morris Neon Laboratories, 1929, collection of the John Crerar Library, University of Chicago; (right) Signs of the Times, May 1956.

20 (left) Signs of the Times, October 1924, 47; (right) Signs of the Times, 1926–1927 various numbers, ST Media Group, used with permission.

21 Author's collection.

22 Collection of Steven Higger, United Sign Systems.

23 (left) Signs of the Times, July 1932, ST Media Group, used with permission; (right) "Diamond Neon Signs," catalog of the Chicago Sign Sales Corp. Charlotte, NC: Chicago Sign Sales Corp, c. 1930. Collection of Avery Library, Columbia University.

24 (top left) DiLemme, Philip. Luminous Advertising Sketches. Cincinnati: Signs of the Times, 1953. Collection of the American Sign Museum; (top right) Becker, Alf R. 100 Alphabets. Cincinnati:

Signs of the Times, 1940. Collection of the American Sign Museum; (bottom) Collection of Justin Langsner, LaSalle Sign Corp.

25 (right) DiLemme, Philip. Luminous Advertising Sketches. Cincinnati: Signs of the Times, 1953. Collection of the American Sign Museum.

26 Signs of the Times, September 1928, 48.

28 (left) "Neon School of New York." New York: Neon School of New York, c. 1950. Collection of the American Sign Museum; (right) "Glass Working Equipment for Neon Industry." Plainfield, NJ: Haydu Brothers, c. 1960. Collection of the American Sign Museum.

29 (left) Signs of the Times, November 1935, ST Media Group, used with permission.

30 "Advertising Run Mad," Municipal Affairs, June 1900.

31 Signs of the Times, Jan. 1931, ST Media Group, used with permission.

34 (left) Collection of Andrew S. Dolkart; (right) Author's collection.

35 (left) HarperCollins: Avon, 1947; (right) The Magazine of Light, 1940 No. 8. Collection of the Hall of Electrical History, The Schenectady Museum and Suits-Bueche Planetarium.

36 (left) New York: The World's Fair City, 1939. Collection of Andrew S. Dolkart; (right) Signs of the Times, October 1964, ST Media Group, used with permission.

39 (left) The Magazine of Light, Year End, 1938. Collection of the Hall of Electrical History, The Schenectady Museum and Suits-Bueche Planetarium; (right) The Magazine of Light, Fall 1935. Collection of the Hall of Electrical History, The Schenectady Museum and Suits-Bueche Planetarium.

48 Puck, March 6, 1907.

176–177 Serota Sign Corp.

# INDEX

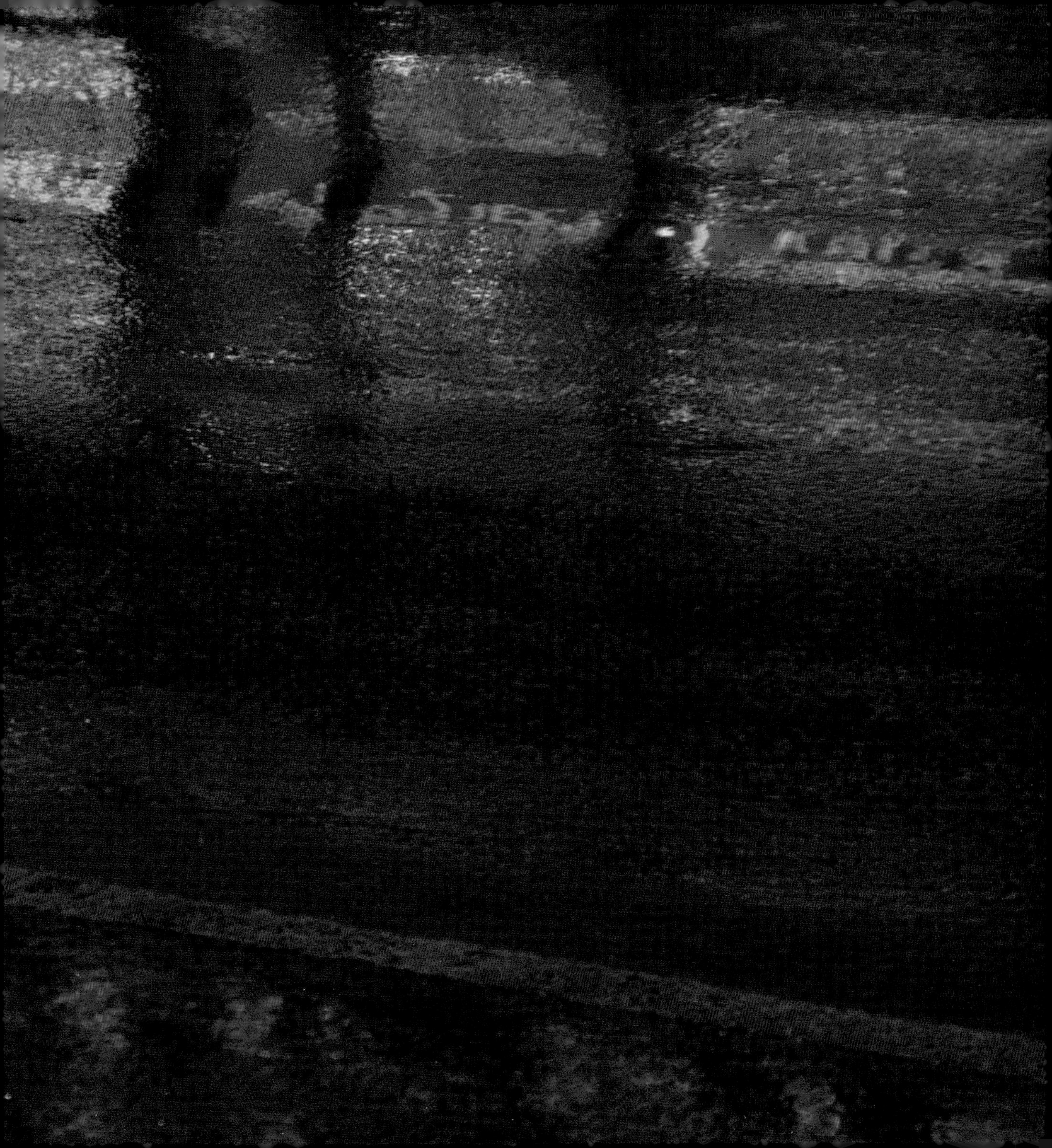

# TREATING NEW YORK CITY AS AN OPEN-AIR MUSEUM,

Thomas E. Rinaldi captures the brilliant glow of surviving early- and mid-twentieth-century neon signs, those iconic elements of the cityscape now in danger of disappearing. This visual tour features two hundred signs, identified by location, with information on their manufacture, date of creation, and the businesses that commissioned them. In a generously illustrated introduction, drawing on documents including rare period trade publications, Rinaldi recounts the development of signage and the technological evolution of neon and examines its role in the streets of New York, in America's cultural identity, and in our collective consciousness.

Raised near Poughkeepsie in upstate New York, **Thomas E. Rinaldi** visited New York City frequently before moving there in 2004. His lifelong interest in the city's built landscape drove him to pursue a career in architecture: he works as a designer for Thornton Tomasetti, a leading engineering and architecture firm. Rinaldi holds degrees in history from Georgetown University and in historic preservation from Columbia University. He is the coauthor, with Robert J. Yasinsac, of *Hudson Valley Ruins: Forgotten Landmarks of an American Landscape.*

Cover design by Modern Good
Cover photographs by Thomas E. Rinaldi

**W. W. NORTON**
NEW YORK · LONDON
www.wwnorton.com

ISBN 978-0-393-73341-9

9 780393 733419

52695

$26.95 USA  $28.50 CAN.